CORDOVA E

D1588248

ROMEO & JULIET: A GUIDE

The Shakespeare Handbooks

ROMEO & JULIET
A Guide

ALISTAIR McCALLUM

Ivan R. Dee
CHICAGO

Library of Congress Cataloging-in-Publication Data:
McCallum, Alistair, 1954–
    Romeo and Juliet : a guide / Alistair McCallum.
      p. cm. — (The Shakespeare handbooks)
    ISBN 1-56663-364-8 (acid-free paper) — ISBN 1-56663-365-6 (pbk. : acid-free paper)
    1. Shakespeare, William, 1564–1616. Romeo and Juliet—Handbooks, manuals, etc. I. Title.

PR2831 .M38 2001
822.3'3—dc21   00-066033

Introduction

In many ways, the plays of Shakespeare's time had a great deal in common with the movie scripts of today. Their prime purpose was to entertain. They were often written to tight deadlines and frequently involved collaboration between writers. Constant revision, cutting and rewriting were the norm. Considerations such as the available actors, current political events, and the changing tastes of the public always had to be borne in mind. Particular productions might excite interest and controversy, but plays were regarded as ephemeral and were rarely published in book form. The poet or essayist might produce a slim, finely bound volume in the hope of literary immortality, but the playwright worked and lived firmly in the present. Plays had not yet become literature. Theatregoing was a pleasure, not a duty.

Four hundred years later, a great deal has changed. Shakespeare is no longer simply a popular playwright; he has become a symbol, an icon. His name generates enthusiasm and anxiety in equal measure. Competing armies of literary critics - a profession unknown in Shakespeare's day - are engaged in a ceaseless war over his reputation and the meaning of his work.

I was lucky enough to grow up in Stratford-on-Avon and, as a regular visitor to the Royal Shakespeare Theatre, became familiar with many of the plays. Whatever else Shakespeare might be, he was not intimidating. The mist surrounding the plays gradually cleared; structure, characters, and ideas started to emerge; the creative input of actors, directors and crew became apparent. The better I understood the plays, the more absorbing and meaningful they became. Familiarity certainly did not breed contempt.

Without this degree of familiarity, approaching a Shakespeare play can be a daunting business. Where do we look for help? There is certainly no shortage of excellent books that discuss, interpret, and analyze Shakespeare's work. But for most of us the problems in approaching Shakespeare are essentially practical: the complexity of his plots, compounded by the obscurity (to modern ears) of his language. What was entirely missing, it seemed to me, was something to guide readers through these difficulties and give them the confidence to respond freely to the plays. This is what I have attempted to provide with the *Shakespeare Handbooks*. Each book gives a straightforward, detailed account of the plot, scene by scene, with plenty of quotations from the play itself, and help with the more obscure words and phrases. I have also included a handful of comments from writers of diverse periods, backgrounds, and opinions, which I hope readers will find thought-provoking, and a few pertinent facts and figures relating to Shakespeare's life and times.

Of course there is no single correct interpretation of a Shakespeare play. His plays were scripts, after all, for his own acting company, a close-knit group of men who worked together for many years; he wrote no introductions or footnotes, and precious few stage directions. The scenery and costumes, the movements and interactions of characters, the mood of the play—all these aspects, and many more, will always be matters for the imaginative judgment of those staging the play. And above all, the creative responses of spectators and readers will be many, varied, and unpredictable.

Shakespeare is challenging. His plays are rich, profound, and enigmatic. The experience of staging, performing, watching or reading them should be a journey of exploration. I hope that the *Shakespeare Handbooks* will give my readers help and encouragement with the first few steps of that rewarding journey.

ROMEO & JULIET: A GUIDE

Setting the scene

Shakespeare probably wrote *Romeo and Juliet* in the period 1594–1595. He had just turned thirty, and was already developing a formidable reputation as a playwright and poet. He had left his native Stratford-on-Avon for London some five years earlier, and was by now a member of the most prestigious and successful acting company in the capital, his plays receiving acclaim at both the public playhouses and the court of Queen Elizabeth.

Although the play was based on a well-known story, the first performances of *Romeo and Juliet* seem to have caused something of a sensation. This was the first time that a full-scale tragedy had dealt with love. Traditionally, tragedies had taken the downfall of kings and emperors as their theme; love, particularly between young people, was regarded as the subject-matter of comedy. The play's setting, too, was recognisably modern, as opposed to the classical world in which tragedies were normally set.

Play texts were guarded jealously by acting companies. If they were published at all, it was generally many years after their composition, when the company could no longer profit from performances. In an attempt to cash in on the popularity of *Romeo and Juliet*, however, unauthorised copies of the play were printed within a year or two of the first performances: these were probably put together by actors, hired by Shakespeare's company, who had played minor roles in the original production. Full of mistakes, omissions and misunderstandings, this 'pirated' version was soon supplanted when Shakespeare's company authorised publication of the original text, giving us the play that we know today.

In the four centuries since its creation, *Romeo and Juliet* has become one of the world's best-loved plays. It has been performed countless times; it has been translated, adapted, filmed and televised; and it has been the inspiration for a wealth of symphonic music, ballet and opera.

". . . Romeo and Juliet *is as perfectly achieved as anything in Shakespeare's work. It is a flawless little jewel of a play. It has the clear, bright colours, the blend of freshness and formality, of an illuminated manuscript.*"

John Wain, *The Living World of Shakespeare*, 1964

A family feud afflicts Verona

The Italian city of Verona, ancient, beautiful and prosperous, is blighted by violence.

An age-old feud between two of its noble families, the Montagues and the Capulets, has been smouldering since time immemorial: and the unending hostility erupts, time and again, into aggression, confrontation and brawling. Family members, relatives, servants, friends and allies are all drawn into the conflict, and at times the quarrelling between the households has spilt over into sporadic street fighting and outright civil disorder.

It is now July. In the long, hot days of midsummer, a menacing air hangs over the city streets: the feud is never far away.

CURTAIN UP

A premonition of tragedy

The Chorus recounts the tragedy which is to come.

The feud between the warring families of Montague and Capulet will only end, he foretells, with the death of their children, destined to take their own lives:

Chorus
From forth the fatal loins of these two foes
A pair of star-cross'd lovers take their life,
Whose misadventur'd piteous overthrows
Doth with their death bury their parents' strife.

Sampson is spoiling for a fight

I, i

Two servants of the Capulet household, Sampson and Gregory, are on the streets of Verona, armed and ready for trouble. In their banter there is an undercurrent of violence and malice, and Sampson boasts of his eagerness to fight.

Gregory points out that the bad blood is between the Montague and Capulet families, not their servants. Sampson shrugs off the distinction; as far as he is concerned, anyone connected with the Montague household is his sworn enemy. Egged on by Gregory, he fantasises of his treatment of the Montagues, his language heavy with innuendo. In Sampson's imagination, his lust for fighting and for rape are almost indistinguishable:

Sampson	. . . I will show myself a tyrant: when I have fought with the men I will be civil with the maids, I will cut off their heads.
Gregory	The heads of the maids?
Sampson	Ay, the heads of the maids, or their maidenheads; take it in what sense thou wilt.
Gregory	They must take it in sense[1] that feel it.
Sampson	Me they shall feel while I am able to stand . . .

[1] *in reality, perceptibly*

Abram and Balthasar, two servants of the Montague household, now appear. Sampson is raring for a fight, but is keen that the blame for starting it should fall on the Montagues. He draws his sword, and tries to tempt his opponents to anger by making an insulting gesture, but without success:

Sampson	. . . I will bite my thumb at them, which is disgrace to them if they bear it.
Abram	Do you bite your thumb at us, sir?
Sampson	I do bite my thumb, sir.
Abram	Do you bite your thumb at us, sir?
Sampson	[*To Gregory.*] Is the law of our side if I say ay?
Gregory	No.
Sampson	No sir, I do not bite my thumb at you, sir, but I bite my thumb, sir.

Montague's men, though hostile, do not respond. Sampson tries again. His master Capulet is as good a man as Montague, he tells Abram aggressively. Again the others refuse to rise to the bait, and the uneasy standoff continues. Emboldened by the approach of Tybalt, a member of the Capulet family, Gregory urges his friend to claim that Lord Capulet is the better man. Sampson does so: Abram accuses him of lying: and the tension erupts into violence, all four men drawing their swords and laying into their opponents.

> "*If* Romeo and Juliet *is the most romantic of Shakespeare's plays, it is also, from the opening episode with its ribald jesting between Capulet's servants, the bawdiest.*"
>
> Stanley Wells, *Shakespeare: A Dramatic Life*, 1994

Rioting breaks out

Benvolio, Lord Montague's nephew, arrives on the scene and immediately calls on the servants to stop fighting. He draws his sword and tries to force the two sides apart: and it is at this moment that Tybalt, nephew of Lady Capulet, arrives. Unlike Benvolio, the hot-tempered Tybalt has no inclination towards peacemaking. His hatred for the Montagues is intense, and he is glad of this opportunity to attack his enemy. He draws his sword and lunges at Benvolio, who is forced to defend himself.

The commotion has by now attracted the attention of the populace. The citizens of Verona gather round, some joining the fray on one side or the other, armed with whatever clubs, axes and spears they can lay their hands on.

Old Lord Capulet himself soon appears, along with his wife. He calls for his sword: Lady Capulet remarks that, at his age, a pair of crutches would be of more use to him. Next on the scene is Lord Montague. As a quarrel flares up between the two old men, Lady Montague sternly orders her husband to keep out of trouble.

Finally, the ruler of Verona, Prince Escalus, approaches with his guards and attendants. The scene of disorder, hostility and violence on the streets of his city fills him with anger and dismay. His first attempt to address the crowd is drowned in the noise and turmoil of the brawl. Raising his voice, he orders them all to drop their weapons, threatening to punish with torture any who do not obey. Order is eventually restored, and the Prince commands the attention of his subjects.

This is not the first time that fighting has broken out in the streets of the city, declares Escalus, and he is well aware of the cause:

Prince   Three civil brawls bred of an airy word
By thee, old Capulet, and Montague,
Have thrice disturb'd the quiet of our streets
And made Verona's ancient citizens
Cast by their grave-beseeming ornaments[1]
To wield old partisans,[2] in hands as old,
Canker'd[3] with peace, to part your canker'd
    hate.

[1] *renounce their suitably dignified behaviour*

[2] *spears, pikes*

[3] *rusty*

The violence must end, announces the Prince: if another public brawl of this kind occurs, he warns, the participants will face the death penalty.

As Prince Escalus leaves, he tells Lord Capulet to accompany him; Lord Montague must appear before him later in the day. He orders the crowd of citizens to disperse peacefully.

> *"Shakespeare has given his magistrate a conscience and a growing presentiment of what must happen to everyone in Verona if the wound in the civil body cannot be healed. Others want to keep the peace, too, but mainly because they have a perfunctory sense of duty, or perhaps because they dislike fighting. Escalus knows from the beginning that keeping the peace here is a matter of life or death."*
>
> J. A. Bryant Jr, Introduction to the Signet Classic edition of *Romeo and Juliet*, 1964

Romeo's parents are anxious

Lord and Lady Montague remain behind with Montague's nephew Benvolio. Montague, worried by the sudden flaring up of the old feud, asks how the disturbance started. Benvolio explains that he had intervened to break up a fight between servants of the two households, that Tybalt had attacked him furiously but ineffectually, and that the fighting had boiled over into the riot they have just witnessed.

Lady Montague is relieved that her son Romeo was not present at the brawl. She asks Benvolio, who is a close friend of Romeo's, whether he has seen her son. Benvolio reveals that early in the morning, in a melancholy mood himself, he was walking through the woods when he caught sight of Romeo: however, the young man, clearly wanting to be alone, disappeared into the woods as soon as he noticed Benvolio.

Lord Montague reflects that Romeo's behaviour has been strange and worrying of late. His son has been seen many times wandering through the gloom before dawn, alone and tearful. Coming home at sunrise, he often shuts himself away in his darkened room:

Lord Montague . . . Away from light steals home my heavy[1] son
And private in his chamber pens himself,
Shuts up his windows, locks fair daylight out
And makes himself an artificial night.

> [1] *sad, listless*

Romeo's parents, and others, have tried to discover the cause of the young man's despair, but so far he has kept his feelings closely guarded:

Lord Montague . . . he, his own affections' counsellor,[1]
        Is to himself - I will not say how true -
        But to himself so secret and so close,
        So far from sounding and discovery,[2]
        As is the bud bit with an envious[3] worm
        Ere he can spread his sweet leaves to the air
        Or dedicate his beauty to the sun.

[1] *revealing his emotions only to himself*
[2] *allowing the depth and nature of his feelings to be known*
[3] *malicious*

Romeo himself now appears. Benvolio asks Lord and Lady Montague to leave the two of them alone together: he will do everything he can to get to the root of the problem. Grateful for his help, and hoping that he will have more success than the others who have tried to talk to Romeo, they hurry away.

Benvolio discovers the truth

Benvolio bids his friend good morning. Romeo is surprised to hear that it is still morning, and complains that time is dragging by too slowly. The cause of Romeo's despair, which has eluded his parents so completely, now becomes plain:

Benvolio	. . . What sadness lengthens Romeo's hours?
Romeo	Not having that which, having, makes them short.
Benvolio	In love?
Romeo	Out.
Benvolio	Of love?
Romeo	Out of her favour where I am in love.
Benvolio	Alas that love so gentle in his view[1]
	Should be so tyrannous and rough in proof.[2]

[1] *in appearance*
[2] *when experienced*

In short, Romeo is hopelessly in love; and the girl he loves is interested neither in love nor in Romeo. As a result, he has become moody and distracted, and, whilst remaining withdrawn in public, has taken to elaborate, poetic expression of his feelings. He rejects Benvolio's sympathy, claiming that it will only add to his burden:

Romeo   . . . This love that thou hast shown
                    Doth add more grief to too much of mine own.
                    Love is a smoke made with the fume of sighs;
                    Being purg'd, a fire sparkling in lovers' eyes;
                    Being vex'd, a sea nourish'd with lovers' tears;
                    What is it else? A madness most discreet,
                    A choking gall, and a preserving sweet.

Romeo asks Benvolio to leave him, but his friend, hoping to help Romeo break free from his obsession, insists on staying by his side.

Benvolio asks the name of Romeo's beloved: but Romeo refuses to utter it, fearing that the pain would be too much to bear. He will only reveal that, to his despair, she has committed herself to a chaste, unmarried life:

Romeo	... O she is rich in beauty, only poor
	That when she dies, with beauty dies her store.[1]
Benvolio	Then she hath sworn that she will still[2] live
	chaste?
Romeo	She hath, and in that sparing[3] makes huge
	waste.
	For beauty starv'd with her severity
	Cuts beauty off from all posterity.

[1] *the beauty that could be passed on to future generations dies with her*
[2] *always*
[3] *thrift, saving (of her capacity for bearing children)*

Benvolio advises his friend to set aside his infatuation and allow himself at least to look at other women. That would only make matters worse, replies Romeo: the sight of other, less beautiful women can only serve to remind him of the perfection of his beloved.

> *"Like all the plays of this period, it reflects something of that disturbance in Shakespeare's own emotional life, of which the more direct, but far from clear, record is the Sonnets. Shakespeare has been, at the age of thirty or thereabouts, in love, and it has proved a rather serious matter. He has come through the fire and is more or less whole again, no doubt; but he still remains much preoccupied with his puzzling and not altogether satisfactory adventure."*
>
> E. K. Chambers, *Shakespeare: A Survey*, 1904

A disappointment for Paris

I, ii

Old Lord Capulet is talking to Count Paris, a young nobleman of the family of Prince Escalus. Capulet remarks that he and Montague have both been ordered by the Prince to keep the peace: at their age, he reflects, they should be able to put their enmity behind them.

Paris is pleased that the feud between the two respected houses is over. However, he is anxious to discuss a more pressing, personal matter. He has already asked for the hand of Juliet, Lord Capulet's young daughter, in marriage: now he is keen to hear Capulet's decision. The old man's words come as a disappointment:

Paris	But now my lord, what say you to my suit?[1]
Lord Capulet	But saying o'er what I have said before.
	My child is yet a stranger in the world,
	She hath not seen the change of fourteen years.
	Let two more summers wither in their pride
	Ere we may think her ripe to be a bride.

[1] *request*

Juliet, not yet fourteen, is not ready for marriage and motherhood. One reason for Capulet's concern for his daughter is immediately made clear:

Paris	Younger than she are happy mothers made.
Lord Capulet	And too soon marr'd[1] are those so early made.
	Earth hath swallow'd all my hopes but she . . .

[1] *spoilt, aged*

Juliet is Capulet's only surviving child, and he does not want his heiress to face the perils of childbirth at such a young age. Marriage must wait: in the meantime, however, Capulet is happy for Paris to try to win Juliet's affection. In the fullness of time, he hopes, Juliet may choose to marry the Count of her own free will, in which case Capulet will gladly give his consent.

Lord Capulet mentions that there will be a feast at his house this evening, and asks Paris to come. Among the guests will be many beautiful young women:

Lord Capulet   At my poor house look to behold this night
               Earth-treading stars that make dark heaven
                   light.
               Such comfort as do lusty young men feel
               When well-apparell'd April on the heel
               Of limping winter treads, even such delight
               Among fresh female buds shall you this night
               Inherit[1] at my house.

     [1] *receive, enjoy*

Juliet, of course, will be amongst those present: but Capulet is keen that Paris should feel free to enjoy the company of all the young women, and should keep an open mind about his choice of future bride.

As the two of them leave, Capulet calls for a servant and hands him the list of guests. He instructs the man to visit all those named in the list, and to invite each one to his house for the evening's festivities.

An unexpected invitation

Before the servant has a chance to speak, Capulet and Paris are gone. The man looks at the list in bewilderment; he cannot read, and will need help before he can set off on his errand.

At this moment Romeo passes by, accompanied by Benvolio, who is still trying to persuade his friend to cure himself of his obsession by turning his attention to other women. The servant approaches and asks for help. Taking Romeo's melodramatic answer literally, he is still unsure whether he has found assistance or not:

Servant	God gi' good e'en; I pray, sir, can you read?
Romeo	Ay, mine own fortune in my misery.
Servant	Perhaps you have learned it without book.[1] But I pray can you read anything you see?

[1] *without reading; by listening and memorising*

Finally the servant establishes that Romeo is genuinely able to read, and he hands him the guest list. Romeo reads out the names, and is curious to know where the gathering is to be held. The servant tells him and, grateful for his help, takes the liberty of inviting the stranger to join them:

Servant	My master is the great rich Capulet, and if you be not of the house of Montagues I pray come and crush a cup of wine.

The servant hurries off to summon the guests. Benvolio is delighted by the chance encounter that has just occurred; for among the guests is Capulet's niece Rosaline. As Benvolio has by now discovered, this is the very girl with whom Romeo is so besotted.

Benvolio proposes that they should go to the feast to compare Romeo's beloved with the other young women; the comparison may even make him change his mind about Rosaline's perfection. Romeo fervently declares that such faithlessness is unthinkable:

Benvolio	At this same ancient[1] feast of Capulet's
	Sups the fair Rosaline, whom thou so loves,
	With all the admired beauties of Verona.
	Go thither and with unattainted[2] eye
	Compare her face with some that I shall show
	And I will make thee think thy swan a crow.
Romeo	When the devout religion of mine eye
	Maintains such falsehood, then turn tears to
	fire . . .

[1] *traditional, time-honoured*
[2] *impartial*

Romeo agrees to go to the feast with Benvolio: but his only pleasure, he insists, will be to relish the sight of his adored Rosaline.

The Nurse reminisces

I, iii

Lady Capulet wishes to have a word with her daughter Juliet. She asks the Nurse - who has been nanny, wet nurse, caretaker and companion since Juliet's infancy - to call for her.

When Juliet arrives, Lady Capulet asks the Nurse to leave them; the subject she wishes to broach with her daughter is confidential. However, no sooner has she sent the Nurse off than she calls her back again, deciding that the Nurse too should hear what she has to say. She starts by raising the matter of Juliet's age.

The Nurse latches on to the subject eagerly, keen to recollect every last detail. First she recalls the birth of her own daughter Susan, born at the same time as Juliet but now dead:

Nurse . . . Come Lammas Eve[1] at night shall she be
        fourteen.
        Susan and she - God rest all Christian souls -
        Were of an age. Well, Susan is with God;
        She was too good for me.

[1] *July 31st, the day before Lammas (a harvest festival, at which loaves made from the first ripe corn are consecrated)*

As she thinks back, another event comes to the Nurse's mind, one that happened on the very day that she had decided to wean the infant Juliet from breast-milk:

Nurse   'Tis since the earthquake now eleven years,
And she was wean'd - I never shall forget it -
Of all the days of the year upon that day.
For I had then laid wormwood to my dug,[1]
Sitting in the sun under the dovehouse wall.
. . . Shake! quoth the dovehouse.[2] 'Twas no need,
    I trow,
To bid me trudge.[3]
And since that time it is eleven years.

[1]   *put bitter oil on my nipple (to put the child off breast-feeding)*
[2]   *the dovehouse shook*
[3]   *there was no need to urge me to run off*

'Tis since the earthquake now eleven years . . .

The Nurse's recollection might well have rung true for the play's original audience. There had been a number of major earthquakes in England within living memory, including one in 1584, some eleven years before the first performances of *Romeo and Juliet*. Scholarly attempts to find evidence of an earthquake in Verona are almost certainly misguided; Shakespeare's Verona, like his Venice, his Athens and his Bohemia, is firmly rooted in Elizabethan England.

The loquacious Nurse, now well into her stride, remembers another little episode from the same time, when a bawdy remark from her husband had an unexpected response from the innocent child:

Nurse   . . . even the day before, she broke her brow,[1]
And then my husband - God be with his soul,
A[2] was a merry man - took up the child,
'Yea', quoth he, 'dost thou fall upon thy face?
Thou wilt fall backward when thou hast more
    wit,
Wilt thou not, Jule?' And by my holidame,
The pretty wretch left crying and said 'Ay'.
. . . I warrant, and[3] I should live a thousand
    years
I never should forget it.

[1] *fell and banged her forehead*
[2] *he*
[3] *if*

The Nurse is so pleased with the anecdote that, despite Lady Capulet's protestations, she repeats the punch line twice, helpless with laughter.

Lady Capulet has ambitions for her daughter

The Nurse's chattering finally comes to an end, and Lady Capulet now raises the subject that is on her mind. She knows of Count Paris's interest in Juliet, and unlike her husband has no qualms about pressing ahead with such an excellent match as soon as possible. Her question takes the young girl by surprise, although the Nurse is proud of the aptness of her response:

Lady Capulet   Tell me, daughter Juliet,
        How stands your dispositions to be married?
Juliet   It is an honour that I dream not of.

Nurse	An honour. Were not I thine only nurse
	I would say thou hadst suck'd wisdom from thy
	teat.
Lady Capulet	Well, think of marriage now. Younger than you
	Here in Verona, ladies of esteem,
	Are made already mothers.
	. . . Thus then in brief:
	The valiant Paris seeks you for his love.

The Nurse, excitable about marriage in general, is almost speechless with enthusiasm for the noble young kinsman of the Prince. Lady Capulet's praise is more measured as she asks Juliet, gently but insistently, whether her feelings are favourable:

Nurse	A man, young lady. Lady, such a man
	As all the world - why, he's a man of wax.[1]
Lady Capulet	Verona's summer hath not such a flower.
Nurse	Nay, he's a flower, in faith a very flower.
Lady Capulet	What say you, can you love the gentleman?

[1] *faultless, perfect*

Lady Capulet asks Juliet to observe the Count closely at this evening's feast, and to note his agreeable good looks. All that is lacking to make him whole and perfect is a wife:

Lady Capulet   Read o'er the volume of young Paris' face
And find delight writ there with beauty's pen.
Examine every married lineament[1]
And see how one another[2] lends content;
And what obscur'd in this fair volume lies,
Find written in the margent[3] of his eyes.
This precious book of love, this unbound lover,
To beautify him only lacks a cover.

[1] *harmoniously matched feature*
[2] *one feature to another*
[3] *margin*

Lady Capulet asks again whether Juliet is ready to accept Paris's love. Juliet, obedient but cautious, promises to look favourably at the young man during the evening's festivities.

The discussion is interrupted as a servant rushes in. The feast has already started and all three ladies have been requested, one way or another, to attend:

Servant   Madam, the guests are come, supper served up,
you called, my young lady asked for, the
Nurse cursed in the pantry, and everything
in extremity. I must hence to wait . . .

The servant hurries off again. With a few final encouraging words for Juliet from the older women, the three of them leave to join the party.

"Oceans of ink were spilt in England during the turmoil of the Reformation over the status of the married life, the rights of lovers, and the interest of parents in their children's matings. The consensus was that parents did indeed have some say in how their children disposed of themselves, but no parent could force a child to marry against its will or refuse a match which was otherwise suitable. In such cases the children could have redress to the ecclesiastical authorities. The common people were scandalized by the dynastic marriages arranged by the nobility who disposed of their children as if they had been so many cattle and sheep, especially when so many of the marriages clapped up with wards of the Crown later came to violent or adulterous ends."

Germaine Greer, *Shakespeare*, 1986

Three guests linger outside

I, iv

As planned, Romeo and Benvolio have met by torchlight in the darkness outside Capulet's house. Their aim is to visit the feast and catch a glimpse of Rosaline and the other young women of Verona. With them is their friend Mercutio, a relative of the Prince. They have brought masks; apart from the lack of an official invitation, both Romeo and Benvolio are of the Montague family and, if recognised, might be unwelcome at the gathering of the Capulets and their friends.

Benvolio proposes that they steal in without formalities and join the dancing at once. Romeo, complaining that his lovesickness leaves him without the will to dance or enjoy himself, intends to stand aside and carry the burning torch. Mercutio tries to persuade him to change his mind, but Romeo, although ready to engage in some light-hearted wordplay, remains resolute:

Romeo	. . . Being but heavy[1] I will bear the light.
Mercutio	Nay, gentle Romeo, we must have you dance.
Romeo	Not I, believe me. You have dancing shoes
	With nimble soles, I have a soul of lead
	So stakes me to the ground I cannot move.
Mercutio	You are a lover, borrow Cupid's wings
	And soar with them above a common bound.[2]
Romeo	I am too sore enpierced with his shaft
	To soar with his light feathers . . .

[1] *sad, dejected*
[2] *boundary; leap, caper*

The three of them put on their masks, ready to make their entrance. Romeo is hesitant, feeling that it may not be such a good idea to visit the party. He had a dream last night, he tells the others; but before he has a chance to describe it, Mercutio dismisses the idea of attaching importance to dreams.

Mercutio then launches into a wild, fanciful description of the doings of Queen Mab, the fairy believed by the superstitious to deliver dreams to suggestible minds as they sleep. He describes the coach in which she travels through the night:

Mercutio   Her chariot is an empty hazelnut
Made by the joiner squirrel or old grub,[1]
Time out o' mind[2] the fairies' coachmakers;
Her waggon-spokes made of long spinners'[3]
          legs,
The cover of the wings of grasshoppers . . .
Her waggoner a small grey-coated gnat . . .

[1] *woodworm*
[2] *since time immemorial*
[3] *daddy-longlegs*

In her tiny carriage, she goes from one bedchamber to another, turning each sleeper's daytime fantasies into dreams:

Mercutio　　　　　　　　　　　　. . . she gallops night by night
　　　　　Through lovers' brains, and then they dream of
　　　　　　　love;
　　　　　O'er courtiers' knees, that dream on curtsies
　　　　　　straight;[1]
　　　　　O'er lawyers' fingers who straight dream on
　　　　　　fees . . .
　　　　　Sometime she driveth o'er a soldier's neck
　　　　　And then dreams he of cutting foreign throats,
　　　　　Of breaches, ambuscados,[2] Spanish blades,
　　　　　Of healths[3] five fathom deep . . .

[1]　*immediately*
[2]　*ambushes*
[3]　*toasts, drinks*

"Mercutio's defense against dreams gives evidence of his own urge to dream, but it also reveals his fear of giving in to the seething night-time world of unconscious desires associated with the feminine; he prefers the broad daylight world of men fighting and jesting."

Coppélia Kahn, *Coming of Age in Verona*, 1977

Romeo finally succeeds in quelling his friend's lengthy, exuberant monologue. Mercutio argues that he is simply pointing out the absurdity of looking for any significance in dreams.

Benvolio declares that they must all get a move on and make their way into Lord Capulet's house before the party is over. Romeo is still uneasy:

Romeo   . . . my mind misgives
          Some consequence yet hanging in the stars
          Shall bitterly begin his fearful date[1]
          With this night's revels . . .

[1] *starting-date of a contract*

However, he sets his fears aside, and the three masked young
men march heartily towards the party.

The dancing begins

I, v

Inside Capulet's house, supper is over. In the banqueting-hall, the servants are hastily clearing away in preparation for the dancing. A few of them are planning their own party later in the evening, when the bustle is over, and are aiming to smuggle in a couple of unauthorised visitors:

Servant   Away with the joint-stools,[1] remove the court-
           cupboard,[2] look to the plate. Good thou,
           save me a piece of marchpane,[3] and as thou
           loves me, let the porter let in Susan Grindstone
           and Nell . . .

       [1] *wooden stools on which guests sat for supper*
       [2] *sideboard used for storing table-linen and cutlery,*
            and for displaying silver plate
       [3] *marzipan*

Lord and Lady Capulet now lead the guests into the hall. Just as the dancing is about to start, Romeo and his companions enter.

Capulet gives the masked strangers a warm welcome, and urges all the girls to dance with the new arrivals. Masquing - the tradition of making an uninvited appearance at a party, in disguise, and joining the dancing - was something he himself enjoyed in his youth:

Lord Capulet Welcome, gentlemen. I have seen the day
              That I have worn a visor[1] and could tell
              A whispering tale in a fair lady's ear,
              Such as would please. 'Tis gone, 'tis gone . . .

          [1] *mask covering the eyes*

Old Capulet's enjoyment of the festivities is tempered by a sense of nostalgia for his lost youth. Once the music is playing and the dancing is under way, he sits down with his cousin and reflects on the passing years. As the two of them argue about the last time they went masquing, Capulet is dismayed to find that the time has passed even more quickly than he had thought. He is appalled to learn that a friend's son, whom he thinks of as a boy, is already a grown man:

Lord Capulet	'Tis since the nuptial of Lucentio,
	Come Pentecost as quickly as it will,
	Some five and twenty years: and then we masqu'd.
Cousin Capulet	'Tis more, 'tis more, his son is elder, sir:
	His son is thirty.
Lord Capulet	Will you tell me that?
	His son was but a ward[1] two years ago.

[1]   *minor*

Romeo, meanwhile, stands spellbound at the edge of the gathering. He has just caught sight of a radiantly beautiful young girl: he watches, transfixed with love, as she moves through the room, standing out so brightly from the crowd. He instantly forgets Rosaline in the passion that sweeps over him. The girl's ethereal beauty seems to him too precious for the real world:

Romeo	O, she doth teach the torches to burn bright.
	It seems she hangs upon the cheek of night
	As a rich jewel in an Ethiop's[1] ear -
	Beauty too rich for use, for earth too dear.
	. . . Did my heart love till now? Forswear it, sight.
	For I ne'er saw true beauty till this night.

[1]   *Ethiopian, ebony-skinned African*

Eager to know who she is, Romeo asks a passing servant, but the man does not know. Undeterred, he resolves to approach the beautiful young woman as soon as the dancing stops.

O, she doth teach the torches to burn bright.

The motif of light occurs more frequently in *Romeo and Juliet* than in any other play by Shakespeare:

"*In* Romeo and Juliet *the beauty and ardour of young love are seen by Shakespeare as the irradiating glory of sunlight and starlight in a dark world. The dominating image is light, every form and manifestation of it: the sun, moon, stars, fire, lightning, the flash of gunpowder . . . There can be no question, I think, that Shakespeare saw the story, in its swift and tragic beauty, as an almost blinding flash of light, suddenly ignited, and as swiftly quenched.*"

Caroline Spurgeon, *Shakespeare's Imagery*, 1935

Tybalt bears a grudge

Romeo's words to the servant are overheard by Tybalt, Lady Capulet's hot-tempered nephew. He recognises Romeo's voice, and is infuriated at the secret entry of a Montague into the Capulet household. He orders a young boy to bring him his rapier; as far as he is concerned, Romeo's provocative action demands immediate retribution.

Lord Capulet notices his nephew's rage, and asks him what has brought it about. When he learns the cause, he asks Tybalt to remain calm and friendly. Romeo's behaviour is courteous and gentlemanly; besides, says Capulet, Romeo's reputation in Verona is impeccable, and he will not have the young Montague mistreated under his roof.

Tybalt objects wilfully, and Lord Capulet in turn loses his temper at the young man's lack of respect:

Lord Capulet ... Show a fair presence and put off these frowns,
An ill-beseeming semblance for a feast.

Tybalt It fits when such a villain is a guest:
I'll not endure him.

Lord Capulet He shall be endur'd.
What, goodman[1] boy! I say he shall! Go to,
Am I the master here or you? Go to.
You'll not endure him! God shall mend my soul,
You'll make a mutiny among my guests,
You will set cock-a-hoop,[2] you'll be the man![3]

[1] ill-bred, common
[2] create havoc
[3] give the orders

Tybalt, still burning with resentment, reluctantly agrees to leave Romeo alone. Nevertheless, Tybalt promises himself, the young Montague will one day be sorry for his intrusion at the Capulets' feast.

"There is a jealousy in hating too: we want to have our enemy to ourselves."
Friedrich Nietzsche, Nachgelassene Fragmente, 1882

A moment of euphoria

Romeo is blissfully unaware of Tybalt's fury, and indeed of everything except the presence of the beautiful girl who caught his eye a few minutes ago. Approaching her, he takes her hand without hesitation. His first words to her, while apologetic and reverential, are also unmistakably amorous:

Romeo	If I profane with my unworthiest hand
	This holy shrine,[1] the gentle[2] sin is this:
	My lips, two blushing pilgrims, ready stand
	To smooth that rough touch with a tender kiss.

[1] *your hand*
[2] *lesser*

Juliet, delighted by the sudden encounter, playfully continues the theme. If he is indeed a devotee, he is entitled to touch the hand of his chosen saint's statue:

Juliet	Good pilgrim, you do wrong your hand too much,
	Which mannerly devotion shows in this;
	For saints have hands that pilgrims' hands do touch,
	And palm to palm is holy palmer's[1] kiss.

[1] *pilgrim bearing a palm leaf to signify that he has visited Jerusalem*

If the palms of worshipper and saint can meet, urges Romeo, so can their lips: and the next moment they are joined in a tender kiss. A second kiss quickly follows, but the encounter is brought to a sudden end by the arrival of the Nurse, who calls Juliet over to talk to her mother.

When Juliet has left, Romeo discovers from the Nurse that the girl he has just met, who has so enchanted him, is none other than the only daughter and heiress of Lord and Lady Capulet. He is devastated: his love, he fears, is bound to have terrible consequences.

At this moment Benvolio comes to fetch Romeo: the excitement is at its peak, he says, and this is the best time to leave. Romeo agrees, but for him Benvolio's words have a more ominous meaning. The sudden joy of his love for Juliet is already marred by the discovery of her identity:

Benvolio	Away, be gone, the sport is at the best.
Romeo	Ay, so I fear; the more is my unrest.

Lord Capulet is sorry to see the three young men go, and decides to bring the party to an end. As the masked youths leave, Juliet sends her Nurse to ask the name of the one who carried the torch, praying desperately that he is not already married.

The truth comes as even more of a shock when the Nurse returns to tell her that he is Romeo, son of the Montagues. But Juliet is in love now, for the first time, and she knows that it is too late to deny her feelings:

Juliet	My only love sprung from my only hate.
	Too early seen unknown, and known too late.
	Prodigious[1] birth of love it is to me
	That I must love a loathed enemy.

[1] *ominous, inauspicious*

Juliet reveals her feelings

II, i - ii

Romeo has left the party in low spirits, dismayed at the discovery of Juliet's identity. However, as he walks away from Capulet's house, the urge to return and to be close to Juliet is overwhelming. In the darkness, he slips away from his two companions and runs back towards the house:

Romeo   Can I go forward when my heart is here?
Turn back, dull earth,[1] and find thy centre out.

[1] *body of foolish, sluggish clay*

Approaching Capulet's house, Romeo comes to a high wall: undeterred, he leaps up it and lowers himself into the orchard on the other side. Benvolio and Mercutio, cheerful and boisterous after their brief invasion of the feast, call out for Romeo. They tease him loudly about his love for Rosaline, unaware of his encounter with Juliet, before giving up the search and setting off home.

Alone in the darkness of the orchard, Romeo looks up at Capulet's house. Suddenly a window opens. Light from within the house floods out, and the radiant figure of Juliet appears:

Romeo   But soft, what light through yonder window breaks?
It is the east and Juliet is the sun!

> ". . . *Romeo has leaped the orchard wall, into another world of unknown joy. A distinct and separate atmosphere and rhythm is established by sudden contrast, as the laughter of the two young men fades away and Romeo stands silently in darkness gazing at the house. Juliet's appearance at a window is the dawn in a rival world . . .*"
>
> Brian Gibbons, Introduction to the Arden edition of *Romeo and Juliet*, 1980

As Juliet gazes out into the darkness, Romeo watches longingly, wishing that she knew of his love, and yearning to be close to her:

Romeo   See how she leans her cheek upon her hand.
              O that I were a glove upon that hand,
              That I might touch that cheek.

Unaware of Romeo's presence in the garden below, Juliet speaks her thoughts wistfully into the night air. To Romeo's amazement and delight, her words reveal that she is as deeply in love with him as he is with her. Like him, Juliet is in anguish over the enmity between their families:

Juliet   O Romeo, Romeo, wherefore[1] art thou Romeo?
              Deny thy father and refuse thy name.
              Or if thou wilt not, be but sworn my love
              And I'll no longer be a Capulet.

              [1]   *why*

Romeo is unsure whether or not he should reveal his presence. As he hesitates, Juliet continues to lament the folly of attaching importance to a family name:

Juliet	'Tis but thy name that is my enemy:
	Thou art thyself, though not[1] a Montague.
	. . . What's in a name? That which we call a rose
	By any other word would smell as sweet . . .

[1] *even if you were not*

Romeo now breaks his silence, announcing impetuously that he will gladly give up his name: to be loved by her is the only identity he needs.

> "Perfect love casteth out fear . . ."
>
> First Epistle of John, King James Bible, 1611

Promises of love

Hearing a voice, Juliet is startled to discover that her secret words have been overheard, and demands to know who has been listening down in the darkness. She soon recognises Romeo's voice, and is astonished that he has managed to scale the high wall around the orchard. He is in terrible danger, she warns, but Romeo insists that his love has made him fearless. The only thing that could cause him pain would be Juliet's indifference:

Romeo	With love's light wings did I o'erperch these walls,
	For stony limits cannot hold love out,
	And what love can do, that dares love attempt:[1]
	Therefore thy kinsmen are no stop to me.
Juliet	If they do see thee, they will murder thee.
Romeo	Alack, there lies more peril in thine eye
	Than twenty of their swords.

[1] *a lover has the courage to attempt anything that is humanly possible*

Juliet asks Romeo who told him where to find her. He asked no-one, he replies, and did not know the way to her window. Guided by his love, though, no journey would be too difficult or too hazardous:

Romeo	I am no pilot,[1] yet wert thou as far
	As that vast shore wash'd with the farthest sea,
	I should adventure[2] for such merchandise.

[1] *navigator, helmsman*
[2] *risk the voyage*

Knowing that Romeo has overheard her secret declaration of love, Juliet realises that there is no point in pretending to be hesitant. In other circumstances, she tells him, she might have shown more restraint; as it is, she is ready to accept Romeo's love immediately and wholeheartedly, and pledges her own faithful, constant love for him. The speed with which they have met, fallen in love and promised their devotion gives Juliet a moment's anxiety:

Juliet   Although I joy in thee,
              I have no joy of this contract tonight:
              It is too rash, too unadvis'd, too sudden,
              Too like the lightning, which doth cease to be
              Ere one can say 'It lightens'.

   Juliet is confident, though, that their love will grow and flourish. She knows that her feelings for Romeo are genuine and profound:

Juliet   My bounty[1] is as boundless as the sea,
              My love as deep: the more I give to thee
              The more I have, for both are infinite.

              [1]   *capacity for giving*

There is a widespread and enduring belief that *Romeo and Juliet* is a true story. In fact there is no evidence that the events described in the play actually happened, although situations of this kind have undoubtedly arisen throughout history; the theme of lovers trying to overcome the hostility of their families is found in folklore and literature from cultures as diverse as ancient Greece and 16th-century Japan.

In his version of the legend, the Italian writer Luigi Da Porto, writing some sixty years before Shakespeare, was the first to give his lovers the names Romeo and Juliet and to set the story in Verona. He also made the claim, common among storytellers of the time, that his was a true account of events. Many adaptations and translations of Da Porto's story were produced, and the tale of the two lovers was very popular in Shakespeare's day, and widely believed to be true.

The people of Verona seem to have welcomed the association

A voice is heard from within the house: it is Juliet's Nurse calling for her to go to bed. Juliet goes in to pacify her for a few minutes, then returns to the window. She intends to send a messenger to Romeo tomorrow, she tells him hurriedly; if he is as much in love as he says, and if he is ready for marriage, he must arrange the ceremony in the morning and give word to her messenger.

Again Juliet is called inside by her Nurse, and again she manages to escape for a few more minutes with Romeo. She knows he must leave. Dawn is breaking, and he is in danger of being discovered, but she is unwilling to let him go:

of their city with the famous love story, and to have encouraged the belief in its historical accuracy; to this day, tour guides in Verona will proudly point out the very balcony from which Juliet addressed her beloved Romeo. Visiting Verona in 1846, a sympathetic but sceptical Charles Dickens describes a visit to the supposed site of Shakespeare's tragedy:

"I went off, with a guide, to an old, old garden: and being admitted, at a shattered gate, by a bright-eyed woman who was washing clothes, went down some walks where fresh plants and young flowers were prettily growing among fragments of old wall, and ivy-covered mounds; and was shown a little tank, or water-trough, which the bright-eyed woman, drying her arms upon her kerchief, called 'la tomba di Giulietta la sfortunata'. With the best disposition in the world to believe, I could do no more than believe that the bright-eyed woman believed; so I gave her that much credit, and her customary fee in ready money."

Juliet	'Tis almost morning, I would have thee gone,
	And yet no farther than a wanton's[1] bird,
	That lets it hop a little from his hand . . .
Romeo	I would I were thy bird.
Juliet	Sweet, so would I:
	Yet I should kill thee with much cherishing.[2]
	Good night, good night. Parting is such sweet
	sorrow
	That I shall say good night till it be morrow.

[1] *a playful, teasing child*
[2] *cosseting and caressing*

Finally, Juliet leaves the window and returns to her room. Romeo clambers out of the orchard and sets off with just one aim in mind: to arrange his marriage to Juliet without delay.

An unexpected request for Friar Laurence

II, iii

Friar Laurence is preparing to leave his monastic cell. Carrying his willow basket, he is about to set out, in the pale light before sunrise, to gather medicinal herbs and flowers while they are still damp with dew.

The Friar reflects on the variety and profusion of plants that spring from the earth, every one of which is beneficial in some way. However, just as good can be found in the meanest of the earth's products, it is equally true, he muses, that even the most wholesome can have unpleasant and dangerous effects if misused:

Friar Laurence O, mickle[1] is the powerful grace that lies
　　　　　　In plants, herbs, stones, and their true qualities.
　　　　　　For naught so vile that on the earth doth live
　　　　　　But to the earth[2] some special good doth give;
　　　　　　Nor aught so good but, strain'd[3] from that fair
　　　　　　　　use,
　　　　　　Revolts from true birth, stumbling on abuse.

[1] *great, abundant*
[2] *to the earth's inhabitants*
[3] *perverted, misapplied*

As Romeo enters the cell, unseen, the Friar singles out a little flower from his collection of medicines. Its odour serves as a useful stimulant: but if it is eaten, it brings the heart to a standstill and causes immediate unconsciousness. This potential for good and evil is present in humanity as well as plants, he reflects:

Friar Laurence Two such opposed kings encamp them still[1]
         In man as well as herbs: grace and rude will;[2]
         And where the worser is predominant
         Full soon the canker[3] death eats up that plant.

    [1] *are permanently resident*
    [2] *base, selfish desires*
    [3] *destructive, parasitical worm*

At this point Romeo greets Friar Laurence, who is surprised to see him up so early. At his age, he should not be suffering from sleeplessness unless he is deeply worried about something: perhaps, suggests the Friar, he has not been in bed at all. Romeo confirms cheerfully that the Friar's guess is correct, and starts on a playful description of the night's events, suggesting that the Friar's healing abilities will be needed:

Romeo   I have been feasting with mine enemy,
         Where on a sudden one hath wounded me
         That's by me wounded. Both our remedies
         Within thy help and holy physic[1] lies.

    [1] *medicine, curative powers*

The Friar tells him to speak plainly, and Romeo comes to the point: he and Juliet are in love, and are determined to be wed as soon as possible. He has come to ask the Friar to marry them later this very day. Friar Laurence is astonished: until now, the young man's talk has all been of Rosaline and the agony of unrequited love. The suddenness of the change in his affections is hardly a promising sign of constancy. Nevertheless, on consideration the Friar agrees to the marriage, hoping that it may bring the feuding between their two families to an end. Romeo is in a hurry to complete the arrangements, but Friar Laurence advises him to take his time:

Friar Laurence   . . . this alliance may so happy prove
             To turn your households' rancour to pure love.
Romeo   O let us hence: I stand on[1] sudden haste.
Friar Laurence Wisely and slow; they stumble that run fast.

[1] *insist on*

"*Rosaline's Romeo is a melancholy, heavy, idle dreamer, wholly absorbed in his own frosty reflections on the matter of love . . . Juliet's Romeo, on the other hand, is a cheerful, lively youth, of a sparkling mind and wit.*"

Hermann Ulrici, *Shakespeare's Dramatic Art*, 1847

Mercutio holds forth

II, iv

The morning after the party, Benvolio and Mercutio have met up again in the streets of Verona. They wonder what has become of their friend Romeo: Benvolio has visited his father's house, but Romeo is not in, and has not been seen since yesterday. His infatuation with the unattainable Rosaline is the cause of Romeo's erratic behaviour, says Mercutio, claiming that it will eventually drive him mad.

Benvolio mentions that a letter from Tybalt had been delivered to the Montagues' house, no doubt a challenge after Romeo's presence at the Capulets' feast. Mercutio is scornful; Tybalt is known for his preoccupation with the technicalities of duelling, and has learnt all the jargon, but is not a spirited fighter:

Mercutio   O, he's the courageous captain of compliments:[1]
he fights as you sing pricksong,[2] keeps time,
distance and proportion . . . Ah, the immortal
passado, the punto reverso . . .

[1]   *master of the etiquette of duelling*
[2]   *singing from printed music, with attention to
accuracy*

Carried away with his verbal onslaught, Mercutio turns his attention to affected, foppish behaviour in general, and starts to warm to the role of outraged old fogey despite his youth:

rjoyed that the marriage is to go ahead, now becomes
e and confiding. She is about to recount an episode from
childhood, but checks herself, only to launch into some
et gossip about Juliet's other suitor:

> Well, sir, my mistress is the sweetest lady. Lord,
> Lord! When 'twas a little prating thing - O,
> there is a nobleman in town, one Paris, that
> would fain lay knife aboard;[1] but she, good
> soul, had as lief[2] see a toad, a very toad, as see
> him. I anger her sometimes and tell her that
> Paris is the properer man, but I'll warrant you,
> when I say so she looks as pale as any clout . . .[3]

[1] *is keen to secure his place at the table*
[2] *as soon*
[3] *cloth, sheet*

> Nurse is one of the characters in which the author de-
> ed; he has, with great subtilty of distinction, drawn her
> ce loquacious and secret, obsequious and insolent, trusty
> dishonest."
>
> ohnson, *The Plays of William Shakespeare*, 1765

ugh the Nurse has a poor grasp of the niceties of lan-
e is enthusiastic about Juliet's lyrical praise of her

| Mercutio | The pox of such antic lisping affecting phantasimes, these new tuners of accent . . .[1] Why, is not this a lamentable thing, grandsire, that we should be thus afflicted with these strange flies,[2] these fashion-mongers . . . who stand so much on the new form that they cannot sit at ease on the old bench? |

[1] *those who adopt new-fangled ways of speaking*
[2] *parasites, dilettantes*

Romeo now comes to join his two friends. They are delighted
to find that he is in high spirits, and no longer tormenting himself with his love for Rosaline. After some amicable banter, Mercutio remarks that love, unlike friendship, makes a man
ridiculous:

| Mercutio | Why, is not this better now than groaning for love? Now art thou sociable, now art thou Romeo; now art thou what thou art, by art[1] as well as by nature. For this drivelling love is like a great natural that runs lolling up and down[2] to hide his bauble[3] in a hole. |

[1] *wit, brightness*
[2] *an idiot who runs to and fro with his tongue hanging out*
[3] *toy, trinket*

As the three of them tease one another good-humouredly, a
rotund, billowing figure, with a manservant in tow, comes into
view. It is Juliet's Nurse.

> "*Mercutio implies that all the extravagant posturing of courtly love hides a simple human urge to copulate.*"
>
> Germaine Greer, *Shakespeare*, 1986

A go-between arrives

The teasing continues as the Nurse approaches. It is now midday, and Mercutio uses this as an opportunity for some ribald mockery:

Nurse	God ye good morrow, gentlemen.
Mercutio	God ye good e'en,[1] fair gentlewoman.
Nurse	Is it good e'en?
Mercutio	'Tis no less, I tell ye; for the bawdy hand of the dial is now upon the prick[2] of noon.

[1] *afternoon*
[2] *literally, the engraved mark at the top of the dial*

The Nurse eventually manages to explain her mission: she is looking for a young man named Romeo, and wants to talk to him in private. Amused at this peculiar assignation, Mercutio and Benvolio leave, agreeing to meet Romeo again later in the day. Romeo assures the Nurse, affronted by Mercutio's familiarity, that his friend should not be taken too seriously:

Nurse	. . . what saucy merchan full of his ropery?[1]
Romeo	A gentleman, Nurse, th talk, and will speak mo will stand to[2] in a mon

[1] *loose talk*
[2] *fulfil, carry out*

Finally calming down, the Nurse her errand. Juliet has sent her, she tel him a stern but roundabout warning her young mistress:

Nurse	. . . first let me tell ye, a fool's paradise, as they gross kind of behaviour, gentlewoman is young. should deal double with thing to be offered to a

Romeo hardly has time to protest jumps to the desired conclusion: that ourable, and that he is proposing mar

Romeo spells out his message to t able to contain her excitement. Juliet rence's cell this afternoon, on the prete Romeo will meet her at the cell, and married there and then by the Friar. Th secret, and it will be impossible for hir Capulet's house, so Romeo has arrange brought to a secluded spot nearby in a is to come back to collect it, and mu window tonight so that Romeo can be

The Nurse, already developing a fon

and o
talkat
Juliet
indisc

Nurse

gua
bel

Mercutio   The pox of such antic lisping affecting
phantasimes, these new tuners of accent . . .[1]
Why, is not this a lamentable thing,
grandsire, that we should be thus afflicted with
these strange flies,[2] these fashion-mongers . . .
who stand so much on the new form that they
cannot sit at ease on the old bench?

[1] *those who adopt new-fangled ways of speaking*
[2] *parasites, dilettantes*

Romeo now comes to join his two friends. They are delighted
to find that he is in high spirits, and no longer tormenting himself with his love for Rosaline. After some amicable banter, Mercutio remarks that love, unlike friendship, makes a man
ridiculous:

Mercutio   Why, is not this better now than groaning for
love? Now art thou sociable, now art thou
Romeo; now art thou what thou art, by art[1] as
well as by nature. For this drivelling love is
like a great natural that runs lolling up and
down[2] to hide his bauble[3] in a hole.

[1] *wit, brightness*
[2] *an idiot who runs to and fro with his tongue
     hanging out*
[3] *toy, trinket*

As the three of them tease one another good-humouredly, a
rotund, billowing figure, with a manservant in tow, comes into
view. It is Juliet's Nurse.

> "*Mercutio implies that all the extravagant posturing of courtly love hides a simple human urge to copulate.*"
>
> Germaine Greer, *Shakespeare*, 1986

A go-between arrives

The teasing continues as the Nurse approaches. It is now midday, and Mercutio uses this as an opportunity for some ribald mockery:

Nurse	God ye good morrow, gentlemen.
Mercutio	God ye good e'en,[1] fair gentlewoman.
Nurse	Is it good e'en?
Mercutio	'Tis no less, I tell ye; for the bawdy hand of the dial is now upon the prick[2] of noon.

[1] *afternoon*
[2] *literally, the engraved mark at the top of the dial*

The Nurse eventually manages to explain her mission: she is looking for a young man named Romeo, and wants to talk to him in private. Amused at this peculiar assignation, Mercutio and Benvolio leave, agreeing to meet Romeo again later in the day. Romeo assures the Nurse, affronted by Mercutio's familiarity, that his friend should not be taken too seriously:

Nurse	. . . what saucy merchant was this, that was so full of his ropery?[1]
Romeo	A gentleman, Nurse, that loves to hear himself talk, and will speak more in a minute than he will stand to[2] in a month.

[1] *loose talk*
[2] *fulfil, carry out*

Finally calming down, the Nurse comes to the purpose of her errand. Juliet has sent her, she tells Romeo, and she gives him a stern but roundabout warning not to take advantage of her young mistress:

Nurse	. . . first let me tell ye, if ye should lead her in a fool's paradise, as they say, it were a very gross kind of behaviour, as they say; for the gentlewoman is young. And therefore, if you should deal double with her, truly it were an ill thing to be offered to any gentlewoman . . .

Romeo hardly has time to protest before the Nurse joyfully jumps to the desired conclusion: that his intentions are honourable, and that he is proposing marriage.

Romeo spells out his message to the Nurse, who is barely able to contain her excitement. Juliet is to come to Friar Laurence's cell this afternoon, on the pretext of going to confession. Romeo will meet her at the cell, and the two of them will be married there and then by the Friar. The wedding must be kept secret, and it will be impossible for him to come openly to Lord Capulet's house, so Romeo has arranged for a rope ladder to be brought to a secluded spot nearby in an hour's time: the Nurse is to come back to collect it, and must hang it from Juliet's window tonight so that Romeo can be with his new bride.

The Nurse, already developing a fondness for the young man,

and overjoyed that the marriage is to go ahead, now becomes talkative and confiding. She is about to recount an episode from Juliet's childhood, but checks herself, only to launch into some indiscreet gossip about Juliet's other suitor:

Nurse   Well, sir, my mistress is the sweetest lady. Lord, Lord! When 'twas a little prating thing - O, there is a nobleman in town, one Paris, that would fain lay knife aboard;[1] but she, good soul, had as lief[2] see a toad, a very toad, as see him. I anger her sometimes and tell her that Paris is the properer man, but I'll warrant you, when I say so she looks as pale as any clout . . .[3]

[1] is keen to secure his place at the table
[2] as soon
[3] cloth, sheet

> "The Nurse is one of the characters in which the author delighted; he has, with great subtilty of distinction, drawn her at once loquacious and secret, obsequious and insolent, trusty and dishonest."
>
> Dr Johnson, The Plays of William Shakespeare, 1765

Although the Nurse has a poor grasp of the niceties of language, she is enthusiastic about Juliet's lyrical praise of her beloved:

Nurse   . . . Doth not rosemary and Romeo begin both
          with a letter?
Romeo   Ay, Nurse, what of that? Both with an 'R'.
Nurse   Ah, mocker! That's the dog's name . . .[1] I know
          it begins with some other letter; and she hath
          the prettiest sententious of it, of you and
          rosemary, that it would do you good to hear it.

[1] *the sound a dog makes*

With a brief command to her manservant to lead the way,
the Nurse bids Romeo a fond farewell.

"*. . . men ought to beware of this passion, which loseth not only other things, but itself . . . For whosoever esteemeth too much of amorous affection, quitteth both riches and wisdom. . . . They do best, who, if they cannot but admit love,[1] yet make it keep quarter, and sever it wholly from their serious affairs and actions of life.*"

[1] *cannot help falling in love*

Francis Bacon, *Of Love*, 1612

The messenger returns

II, v

Back at Lord Capulet's house, Juliet is waiting impatiently for her Nurse to return with news of Romeo. The Nurse left at nine, promising to be back in half an hour. Three hours have passed since then, and Juliet is becoming increasingly frustrated with the slowness and lack of urgency that seems to come with age:

Juliet	Had she affections and warm youthful blood
	She would be as swift in motion as a ball:
	My words would bandy[1] her to my sweet love,
	And his to me.

> [1] *strike or throw back and forth*

The Nurse finally arrives, exhausted and bad-tempered after her long walk. To Juliet's exasperation, she is too breathless to pass on her news straight away:

Nurse	Fie, how my bones ache. What a jaunce have I![1]
Juliet	I would thou hadst my bones and I thy news.
	Nay come, I pray thee, speak . . .

> [1] *what a journey I've been on*

Despite Juliet's insistence, the Nurse refuses to be hurried. Hurt by her mistress's lack of sympathy, she keeps her waiting, determined that the girl should appreciate how arduous her errand has been. Finally, the Nurse gives Juliet the news she wants to hear, and is amused at the girl's blushes:

Nurse	Have you got leave to go to shrift[1] today?
Juliet	I have.
Nurse	Then hie you hence to Friar Laurence' cell.
	There stays a husband to make you a wife.
	Now comes the wanton[2] blood up in your cheeks.
	. . . I am the drudge, and toil in your delight,
	But you shall bear the burden[3] soon at night.

[1] *permission to go to confession*
[2] *uncontrollable, irrepressible*
[3] *do the work; carry the weight of your husband*

". . . *right and wrong are so interwoven with one another, that the right of the lovers is, at the same time, a wrong, their secret marriage both a moral and an immoral proceeding. The task of the tragic action is to solve this contradiction.*"

Hermann Ulrici, *Shakespeare's Dramatic Art*, 1847

The lovers come together

II, vi

In Friar Laurence's cell, Romeo awaits Juliet's arrival. This day's bliss will more than make up for any sorrows that lie ahead, believes Romeo. The Friar urges him to be restrained in his passion, and to value the pleasures of enduring love:

Romeo   . . . come what sorrow can,
It cannot countervail[1] the exchange of joy
That one short minute gives me in her sight.
Friar Laurence These violent delights have violent ends
And in their triumph die, like fire and powder,[2]
Which as they kiss consume.[3]
. . . Therefore love moderately; long love doth so.
Too swift arrives as tardy as too slow.

[1]   *outweigh*
[2]   *gunpowder*
[3]   *are destroyed*

Juliet, quick and light-footed, now runs in and embraces Romeo. He asks her to speak of her love, but her feelings are too deep to put into words:

Juliet   They are but beggars that can count their
worth,
But my true love is grown to such excess
I cannot sum up sum[1] of half my wealth.

[1]   *count the total*

The Friar leads the two of them away. It is time for the wedding ceremony.

Tybalt seeks out Romeo

III, i

In the oppressive heat of the summer afternoon, there is a sultry, menacing air in the streets of Verona. Benvolio suggests to Mercutio that the two of them should keep out of harm's way:

Benvolio   I pray thee, good Mercutio, let's retire;
        The day is hot, the Capels[1] are abroad,
        And if we meet we shall not 'scape a brawl,
        For now these hot days is the mad blood stirring.

    [1] *Capulets*

Mercutio is unimpressed by his friend's caution, and even accuses the mild-mannered Benvolio of being quarrelsome and belligerent himself. As evidence, he conjures up a series of unlikely scenes that he claims to have witnessed. Benvolio points out that Mercutio should be the last person to make such accusations:

Mercutio   Why, thou wilt quarrel with a man that hath a hair more or a hair less in his beard than thou hast. Thou wilt quarrel with a man for cracking nuts, having no other reason but because thou hast hazel eyes . . . Thou hast quarrelled with a man for coughing in the street, because he hath wakened thy dog that hath lain asleep in the sun . . .

Benvolio   And[1] I were so apt to quarrel as thou art, any man should buy the fee simple[2] of my life for an hour and a quarter.

    [1] *if*
    [2] *anyone could afford to buy complete possession, as my life expectancy would be so short*

The joking is brought to a sudden end as Tybalt appears. Benvolio is apprehensive: Mercutio remains defiant. Tybalt, still smarting from Romeo's appearance at the feast, accuses Mercutio of being a friend of the young Montague. The two of them confront one another aggressively and, despite Benvolio's pleas for calm, the tension quickly grows, and violence seems imminent. However, as the two are about to cross swords, Romeo, the real target of Tybalt's anger, appears.

Tybalt turns away from Mercutio with a curt word of conciliation, and approaches Romeo. The public insult with which he hopes to provoke Romeo to anger has no effect. Romeo is in no mood to fight; indeed, he is enjoying the secrecy which, for the time being, must shroud the marriage which has just taken place between himself and Tybalt's cousin:

Tybalt	Romeo, the love I bear thee can afford No better term than this: thou art a villain.
Romeo	Tybalt, the reason that I have to love thee Doth much excuse the appertaining rage[1] To such a greeting . . .

> [1] *does a great deal to prevent the fitting angry response*

Determined to incite a quarrel, Tybalt calls on Romeo to draw his rapier, but Romeo remains resolutely calm and enigmatic:

Romeo	I do protest I never injuried thee, But love thee better than thou canst devise Till thou shalt know the reason of my love. And so, good Capulet, which name I tender[1] As dearly as mine own, be satisfied.

> [1] *esteem, value*

Mercutio, appalled at his companion's refusal to defend his honour, and still chafing from his earlier confrontation, draws his rapier and calls on Tybalt to fight. More than ready, Tybalt also draws, and the two young men lunge at one another impetuously.

Romeo and Benvolio are horrified: the Prince has expressly forbidden such violent public confrontations, on pain of death. They draw their rapiers and intervene, trying to come between the fighters and beat down their weapons.

While Romeo is holding Mercutio back, his arm outstretched to keep his friend's rapier away from his opponent, Tybalt seizes his opportunity and thrusts viciously at Mercutio while he is off guard. Mercutio falls, and Tybalt runs off hastily.

Mercutio calls for help, and his manservant rushes away to fetch a surgeon. Romeo tries desperately to reassure himself that the wound is slight, but soon realises, mortified and helpless, that his friend is dying. Mercutio is grimly humorous to the last, but it galls him that an uninspired fighter such as Tybalt has got the better of him:

Romeo	Courage, man, the hurt cannot be much.
Mercutio	No, 'tis not so deep as a well, nor so wide as a church door, but 'tis enough, 'twill serve. Ask for me tomorrow and you shall find me a grave man. I am peppered, I warrant, for this world. A plague o' both your houses . . .[1] A braggart, a rogue, a villain, that fights by the book of arithmetic - why the devil came you between us? I was hurt under your arm.
Romeo	I thought all for the best.

[1] *Montagues and Capulets*

> A *plague o' both your houses* . . .
>
> ". . . *it is a dying man's curse, which for the Elizabethans was ominous and certain to be fulfilled. Mercutio's departure immediately darkens the scene and the situation. This is the first death* . . ."
>
> T. J. B. Spencer, Introduction to the New Penguin edition of *Romeo and Juliet*, 1967

Mercutio turns to Benvolio for help, and as the two of them withdraw Romeo is left on his own to reflect on what has happened. He reproaches himself bitterly for not responding to Tybalt's challenge. When Benvolio returns with the news that Mercutio is dead, Romeo predicts sombrely that more suffering will follow:

Romeo   This day's black fate on mo[1] days doth depend:[2]
             This but begins the woe others must end.

     [1] *more*
     [2] *loom over*

Tybalt now returns to the scene, and Romeo turns on him at once, furious and vengeful. They draw their rapiers, and a violent struggle immediately ensues. A few moments later, Tybalt is lying dead on the ground.

Romeo's punishment is pronounced

For a moment Romeo remains motionless, bewildered and horrified at what has happened. Benvolio urges him to snap out of his trance and escape at once. The crowds are gathering, and Romeo risks execution if he is captured:

Benvolio Romeo, away, be gone,
      The citizens are up,[1] and Tybalt slain!
      Stand not amaz'd. The Prince will doom thee
        death[2]
      If thou art taken. Hence, be gone, away!
Romeo   O, I am fortune's fool.[3]

[1] *roused, agitated*
[2] *condemn you to death*
[3] *the object of fortune's malicious sport*

No sooner has Romeo run off than a group of angry citizens approaches, looking for those involved in the brawl. They lay hold of Benvolio, as witness to the killing that has just taken place.

Soon, the disturbance attracts wider attention, and a crowd of onlookers gathers around Tybalt's lifeless body. The Montagues and the Capulets soon approach, and finally the Prince appears, wrathful but subdued.

Prince Escalus demands to know who was responsible for this latest affray. Benvolio tells him that Romeo has killed Tybalt, who himself had just killed the Prince's kinsman Mercutio. Lady Capulet, overcome with grief and anger, calls on the Prince to sentence the young Montague to death at once. The Prince does not respond, but asks Benvolio to continue with his account.

Benvolio describes Romeo's calm response to Tybalt's challenge, and the ensuing fight between Tybalt and Mercutio. He goes on to describe Romeo's attempt to intervene, the cowardly thrust from Tybalt that took Mercutio's life, and the sudden, vengeful rage that drove Romeo to kill Tybalt.

Lady Capulet protests angrily; Benvolio is Lord Montague's nephew, and is giving a distorted version of events. In reality, she claims, Tybalt was set upon and overpowered by a mob, and murdered by Romeo. The death penalty is the only just punishment, she repeats. Montague counters that Tybalt should have died anyway for the murder of Mercutio.

Prince Escalus pronounces his judgement. Romeo is to be exiled from Verona, and both families forced to pay punitive damages:

Lord Montague . . . His fault concludes but what the law should end,
    The life of Tybalt.
Prince   And for that offence
    Immediately we do exile him hence.
    I have an interest in your hearts' proceeding;
    My blood[1] for your rude brawls doth lie
      a-bleeding.
    But I'll amerce[2] you with so strong a fine
    That you shall all repent the loss of mine.[3]

[1] *my relative, Mercutio*
[2] *penalise*
[3] *my own loss*

Romeo must leave at once: there is to be no appeal, and he will be executed if he is ever found in Verona again. The Prince orders Tybalt's body to be carried away.

"Tybalt is a recognisably tragic character . . . he alone takes the feud seriously: it is his inner law, the propeller of his fiery nature. He speaks habitually in the tragic rhetoric of honour and death. Ironically, his imperatives come to dominate the play's world only when he himself departs from it."

Susan Snyder, *Romeo and Juliet: Comedy into Tragedy*, 1970

Juliet's dreams are shattered

III, ii

Juliet has returned home after the secret wedding ceremony. She
is eagerly awaiting the night, and the clandestine visit from
Romeo which they have planned. She calls on the sun to hurry
towards sunset, and for darkness to arrive soon:

Juliet   Gallop apace, you fiery-footed steeds,[1]
     Towards Phoebus' lodging . . .
     Spread thy close curtain, love-performing night,
     That runaway's eyes may wink,[2] and Romeo
     Leap to these arms untalk'd-of and unseen.
     Lovers can see to do their amorous rites
     By their own beauties . . .

> [1] *horses of the chariot of Phoebus, the sun-god,*
> *whose nightly resting place was beneath the*
> *horizon*
> [2] *so that furtive eyes are prevented from seeing*

Juliet is longing for her wedding-night, and the ecstasy of
her first sexual embrace with her new husband:

Juliet   Come night, come Romeo, come thou day in
      night,
     For thou wilt lie upon the wings of night
     Whiter than new snow upon a raven's back.
     Come gentle night, come loving black-brow'd
      night,
     Give me my Romeo; and when I shall die
     Take him and cut him out in little stars,
     And he will make the face of heaven so fine
     That all the world will be in love with night,

And pay no worship to the garish sun.
O, I have bought the mansion of a love
But not possess'd it . . .

Juliet's excited anticipation is interrupted by the arrival of the Nurse. She is carrying the rope ladder, as planned, which was to allow Romeo to be with his bride: however, far from sharing Juliet's excitement, she is overcome with grief.

In her agitation the Nurse is almost incoherent, and at first Juliet is unable to learn the cause of her anguish. For a few agonising moments she fears that Romeo has died, even that he has taken his own life. Finally the Nurse manages to make plain what has happened. Juliet is stunned at the death of her cousin and the treachery of her beloved:

Nurse	Tybalt is gone and Romeo banished.
	Romeo that kill'd him, he is banished.
Juliet	O God! Did Romeo's hand shed Tybalt's blood?
Nurse	It did, it did, alas the day, it did.
Juliet	O serpent heart, hid with a flowering face.
	. . . Was ever book containing such vile matter
	So fairly bound?

The Nurse, calming down a little, calls for some brandy; all this terrible news is making her feel her age, she complains. All men are deceitful and disloyal, she claims, reproaching Romeo bitterly.

Juliet, hearing her husband criticised, immediately leaps to his defence. Her momentary resentment towards Romeo vanishes, and she is ashamed to have spoken ill of him. Convinced that there must be some reason for his action, she decides that he must have killed Tybalt in self-defence. She should be glad, then, that Romeo is alive, rather than sad at Tybalt's death: but suddenly she remembers the final part of the Nurse's news, the awful fact of Romeo's banishment. Romeo is alive; but it dawns on her, with a growing sense of desolation, that she will never see him again.

The Nurse, sympathetic and affectionate again towards her young mistress, reassures Juliet that her husband will be with her tonight. He is still in Verona, in hiding at Friar Laurence's cell, she reveals: she will make her way there at once, and persuade him to join his bride for their wedding-night. Juliet gives her a token to pass on to Romeo as a sign of her enduring love:

Nurse   Hark ye, your Romeo will be here at night.
                I'll to him. He is hid at Laurence' cell.
Juliet   O find him, give this ring to my true knight
                And bid him come to take his last farewell.

"Morally how does Nurse stand? Does one protect, in fact encourage one's child to harbour, a convicted murderer? The answer must be yes, if, like Nurse, one believes that happiness with one's chosen man, however fleeting, is the very essence of life. There have been murderers and deserters since the beginning of history who have gained respite because of the loyalty of their women."

Brenda Bruce on her performance as the Nurse, *Players of Shakespeare*, 1985

Romeo learns of his fate

III, iii

Following the killing of Tybalt, Friar Laurence is sheltering Romeo in his cell. The Friar has ventured out, leaving Romeo in hiding, to learn of the sentence that has been passed on the young man. He now returns with the news. The Prince has been lenient, he explains, and has sentenced him to banishment, not death.

Romeo is devastated at the news, and the Friar's attempts to console him only make him more angry and wretched. Life without Juliet is worthless:

Friar Laurence O deadly sin, O rude unthankfulness . . .
This is dear mercy and thou seest it not.
Romeo 'Tis torture and not mercy. Heaven is here
Where Juliet lives, and every cat and dog
And little mouse, every unworthy thing,
Live here in heaven and may look on her,
But Romeo may not.

The Friar is determined to make Romeo look at his predicament in a calmer, more reasonable frame of mind, but Romeo refuses to listen:

Friar Laurence Thou fond[1] mad man, hear me a little speak.

Romeo   O, thou wilt speak again of banishment.

Friar Laurence I'll give thee armour to keep off that word,
               Adversity's sweet milk, philosophy,
               To comfort thee though thou art banished.

Romeo   Yet[2] 'banished'? Hang up philosophy.
               Unless philosophy can make a Juliet,
               Displant a town, reverse a Prince's doom,[3]
               It helps not, it prevails not. Talk no more.

[1]   *foolish*
[2]   *still*
[3]   *sentence*

Romeo collapses in misery onto the floor. There is a knock at the door, but he refuses to move, ignoring the Friar's pleas that he should hide and avoid arrest. The Friar tries to keep the visitor waiting outside, desperate to ensure Romeo's safety. Eventually he establishes that the caller brings news of Juliet. He opens the door, and the Nurse hurries in. She sees at once that Romeo, like Juliet, is in utter despair, and calls on him to get up from the floor and come to his senses.

Hearing the Nurse's voice, Romeo asks after Juliet, convinced that she must now despise him for the murder of Tybalt. In his self-loathing, he asks the Friar how he can eradicate the name that is so hateful to Juliet, and threatens to take his own life:

Romeo   O, tell me, Friar, tell me,
             In what vile part of this anatomy
             Doth my name lodge? Tell me that I may sack[1]
             The hateful mansion.

[1]   *so that I can destroy*

Friar Laurence now addresses Romeo sternly, reprimanding him for his self-pity and wilfulness. Suicide would be a shameful waste, and would only add to the misery of Juliet, whom he claims to love. He is alive; Juliet is alive; and the Prince has shown clemency. He must stop indulging in wild lamentation:

Friar Laurence A pack of blessings light upon thy back;
               Happiness courts thee in her best array;
               But like a mishav'd[1] and a sullen wench
               Thou pouts upon thy fortune and thy love.
               Take heed, take heed, for such die miserable.

      [1] *misbehaved*

The Friar proposes a plan of action. Romeo is to visit Juliet tonight, as planned, using the rope ladder to climb up to her room. He must leave before the city gates are guarded for the night, or, failing that, disguise himself and set off secretly before daybreak. He must then make his way to Mantua, his place of exile. In due course, the Friar hopes, Romeo's marriage to Juliet can be made public, and Romeo forgiven and welcomed back to Verona. In the meantime, he must resign himself to a life of exile in Mantua:

Friar Laurence . . . Where thou shalt live till we can find a
               time
               To blaze[1] your marriage, reconcile your friends,
               Beg pardon of the Prince and call thee back,
               With twenty hundred thousand times more joy
               Than thou wentst forth in lamentation.

      [1] *proclaim, announce*

Finally, Friar Laurence instructs the Nurse to return and tell Juliet of her husband's imminent arrival. The Nurse, spellbound throughout by the Friar's forthright lecture, prepares to leave at once:

Nurse   O lord, I could have stay'd here all the night
            To hear good counsel. O, what learning is.
            My lord, I'll tell my lady you will come.

Just before she goes, the Nurse remembers the ring that Juliet gave her: she presents it to Romeo, who is greatly comforted.

Friar Laurence assures Romeo that he will be kept informed of any events in Verona that might smooth the path of his eventual return. Romeo, his spirits raised, bids the Friar a grateful farewell and sets off to be with his new bride.

Juliet's future is decided

III, iv

Count Paris has paid a visit to the Capulets. Tybalt's death has been a terrible blow to Juliet, Lord Capulet tells him, and he has not raised the subject of marriage with her. However, Lady Capulet promises to talk to her: it is very late now, and Juliet is to be left alone with her grief, but she will see her daughter in the morning and try to ascertain her feelings.

Just as Paris is leaving, Lord Capulet, on a sudden impulse, calls him back. Setting aside his earlier scruples about Juliet's age and readiness for marriage, he resolves that the matter must be settled urgently, once and for all: Juliet must marry the Count without further delay or discussion. He is sure of her love for Paris; whatever her feelings, though, he is confident that her obedient nature will ensure her agreement to the marriage:

Lord Capulet Sir Paris, I will make a desperate tender[1]
Of my child's love. I think she will be rul'd
In all respects by me; nay, more, I doubt it not.

[1] *risk making an offer*

It is Monday night now: the marriage will take place, declares Capulet after a moment's thought, on Thursday. Despite his love of festivities, he resolves that the celebrations will be kept simple and subdued as a mark of respect for the dead Tybalt. The Count is delighted at the unexpected swiftness of the decision:

Lord Capulet	Do you like this haste?
	We'll keep no great ado - a friend or two.
	For, hark you, Tybalt being slain so late,[1]
	It may be thought we held him carelessly,[2]
	Being our kinsman, if we revel much.
	Therefore we'll have some half a dozen friends
	And there an end. But what say you to
	Thursday?
Paris	My lord, I would that Thursday were tomorrow.

[1] *recently*
[2] *lightly, in low esteem*

Capulet instructs his wife to break the news to Juliet as soon as possible. Time is moving on; they are well into the small hours of the morning, and daybreak is approaching.

"*The character who makes the most impressive entrances in the play is a character we never see, the sun.*"

Northrop Frye, *On Shakespeare*, 1986

Time to part

III, v

Romeo and Juliet have spent their first brief night together as man and wife. It is nearly dawn, and Romeo knows that he must soon set off for Mantua. Juliet tries to persuade him that it is not yet time to go:

Juliet   Wilt thou be gone? It is not yet near day.
                It was the nightingale and not the lark
                That pierc'd the fearful hollow of thine ear.

But Romeo knows that this is just wishful thinking: there are streaks of early morning light in the sky, and the distant mountain-tops are already touched by sunlight. If Juliet wants him to stay, he tells her, he is as ready to stay and face death as leave and face banishment. She too, though, knows that it is time for him to go. Filled with sadness, the two of them prepare to part:

Juliet   O now be gone, more light and light it grows.
Romeo   More light and light: more dark and dark our
                woes.

The Nurse now comes hastily to Juliet's door, and warns her that Lady Capulet is on her way. With a final kiss, Romeo runs to the window and clambers down the rope ladder into the orchard.

As Juliet leans from the window, they exchange a few final loving words. Romeo is confident that they will eventually be together again, but Juliet has a terrible sense of foreboding as she looks down at the shadowy figure in the half-light:

Juliet	O think'st thou we shall ever meet again?
Romeo	I doubt it not, and all these woes shall serve
	For sweet discourses[1] in our times to come.
Juliet	O God, I have an ill-divining[2] soul!
	Methinks I see thee, now thou art so low,
	As one dead in the bottom of a tomb.
	Either my eyesight fails, or thou look'st pale.

[1] *conversations*
[2] *pessimistic, predicting misfortune*

As Romeo disappears into the gloom of the orchard, Lady Capulet enters the room. Juliet, wondering why her mother is up and about so early in the morning, comes away from the window. Lady Capulet is equally surprised that Juliet is out of bed at such an early hour, and notices that she is distressed and tearful.

Lady Capulet concludes that her daughter is still mourning the death of her cousin Tybalt. Rather than grieve any longer, she urges Juliet, her thoughts should be of revenge. Lady Capulet reveals that Romeo's destination has been discovered, and plans to deal with him are already under way:

Lady Capulet	We will have vengeance for it, fear thou not.
	Then weep no more. I'll send to one in Mantua,
	Where that same banish'd runagate[1] doth live,
	Shall give him such an unaccustom'd dram
	That he shall soon keep Tybalt company;
	And then I hope thou wilt be satisfied.

[1] *renegade*

Juliet plays along with her mother's misapprehension, pretending to loathe Romeo for the killing of Tybalt. When speaking of her husband, though, she cannot help but phrase her answers ambiguously:

Juliet   O, how my heart abhors
                    To hear him nam'd, and cannot come to him
                    To wreak the love I bore my cousin
                    Upon his body that hath slaughter'd him.

Lady Capulet, glad that her daughter shares her desire for revenge, now raises the subject that has prompted this early morning visit. She prepares Juliet for the news by emphasising Lord Capulet's concern for her, and his desire to lessen the burden of her grief:

Lady Capulet . . . thou hast a careful[1] father, child;
                    One who to put thee from thy heaviness
                    Hath sorted out[2] a sudden day of joy,
                    That thou expects not, nor I look'd not for.[3]

> [1] *thoughtful, considerate*
> [2] *selected, chosen*
> [3] *I did not dare to hope for*

It has been decided, reveals Lady Capulet, that she and Count Paris are to be married in two days' time.

Lord Capulet is displeased

Juliet is horrified at her mother's news. Making no attempt to hide her dismay, she refuses immediately to give her assent. Her thoughts turn to Romeo, but she quickly disguises her true feelings:

Juliet   I pray you tell my lord and father, madam,
I will not marry yet. And when I do, I swear
It shall be Romeo, whom you know I hate,
Rather than Paris.

At this point Capulet himself comes into the room, along with the Nurse. He is surprised to find Juliet in tears, and assumes, as did his wife earlier, that she is still weeping for her dead cousin. Lady Capulet tells her husband of their daughter's wilful refusal to consent to the marriage. His initial response is incomprehension:

Lord Capulet   . . . Have you deliver'd to her our decree?
Lady Capulet   Ay sir, but she will none, she gives you thanks.
I would the fool were married to her grave.
Lord Capulet   Soft. Take me with you,[1] take me with you,
wife.
How? Will she none? Doth she not give us
thanks?
Is she not proud?

---

[1] *tell me what you mean*

Juliet tries to tell her father that, although she knows his intentions are kind, she feels nothing but loathing for Paris. Lord Capulet is in no mood to tolerate dissent: this marriage will go ahead, he commands, whether she likes it or not.

Juliet kneels down and begs to be heard, but Capulet refuses to listen. Raising his voice, he starts to scold and threaten her so severely that Lady Capulet is shocked. The Nurse too is alarmed, and tries to come to Juliet's defence, but she receives an angry, sarcastic response:

Lord Capulet	Hang thee young baggage, disobedient wretch!
	. . . My fingers itch. Wife, we scarce thought us blest
	That God had lent us but this only child;
	But now I see this one is one too much,
	And that we have a curse in having her . . .
Nurse	God in heaven bless her.
	You are to blame, my lord, to rate[1] her so.
Lord Capulet	And why, my Lady Wisdom? Hold your tongue,
	Good Prudence! Smatter[2] with your gossips, go.

[1] *berate, reprimand*
[2] *chatter*

The Nurse continues to object, and Capulet's rage grows until, in a furious outburst, he declares that he will disown his daughter utterly if she refuses to accept the match for which he has worked so hard:

Lord Capulet	God's bread, it makes me mad! Day, night, work, play,
	Alone, in company, still my care hath been[1]
	To have her match'd . . .
	Thursday is near. Lay hand on heart. Advise.[2]
	And[3] you be mine I'll give you to my friend;
	And you be not, hang! Beg! Starve! Die in the streets!
	For by my soul I'll ne'er acknowledge thee,
	Nor what is mine shall never do thee good.

[1] *my concern has always been*
[2] *consider, reflect*
[3] *if*

Capulet storms out, leaving Juliet grief-stricken and bewildered. She pleads desperately with her mother to delay the marriage to Paris; but Lady Capulet, exhausted and despondent, has had enough of the whole affair. She no longer cares what happens to Juliet, she tells her wearily, and leaves her alone with the Nurse.

A change of loyalties

Juliet can see no way out of her predicament, and begs her Nurse to give her some advice, or at least some words of comfort. The Nurse's response is blunt and unexpected:

Nurse   Romeo is banish'd, and all the world to
               nothing[1]
           That he dares ne'er come back to challenge[2]
               you.
           Or if he do, it needs must be by stealth.
           Then, since the case so stands as now it doth,
           I think it best you married with the County.[3]

           [1] *I'd bet all the money in the world*
           [2] *claim, win*
           [3] *Count Paris*

As her thoughts turn to the noble young Paris, she becomes more and more enthusiastic:

Nurse   O, he's a lovely gentleman.
           Romeo's a dishclout to him.[1] An eagle, madam,
           Hath not so green, so quick, so fair an eye
           As Paris hath. Beshrew my very heart,
           I think you are happy in this second match,
           For it excels your first; or, if it did not,
           Your first is dead, or 'twere as good he were . . .

           [1] *a dishcloth, a rag in comparison to him*

Juliet asks the Nurse calmly if these are her true feelings, and the Nurse assures her that they are. Remaining composed, Juliet asks her to pass on a message to her mother: she is sorry for the displeasure she has caused, and plans to visit Friar Laurence immediately to ask his forgiveness. Pleased at Juliet's apparent change of heart, the Nurse sets off to tell Lady Capulet the good news.

On her own, Juliet gives vent to the scorn and anger that she now feels towards her Nurse. She will ask for the Friar's help; but if there is no other way out, the choice of suicide remains as the final resort:

Juliet   Ancient damnation![1] O most wicked fiend . . .
           Thou and my bosom henceforth shall be twain.[2]
           I'll to the Friar to know his remedy.
           If all else fail, myself have power to die.

           [1] *evil old woman*
           [2] *separated*

A desperate solution

IV, i

Count Paris has come to visit Friar Laurence, to tell him the good news of his forthcoming wedding. The Friar, unable to reveal the truth about Juliet's marriage to Romeo, tries to persuade him that the idea is too hasty and ill-considered: but Paris is undeterred. The wedding is only two days away, and Paris explains that Lord Capulet, in his wisdom, has chosen such an early date to help Juliet forget her grief over the death of her cousin.

To Paris's delight, Juliet herself now arrives at the Friar's cell. He knows nothing of the angry scene that has taken place between Juliet and her parents, and greets her affectionately. Her response is cool and distant, but Paris, in his high spirits, is aware only of the happiness which lies ahead. Juliet asks to be left alone with the Friar, and Paris gives her a fond kiss as he takes his leave.

Friar Laurence tells Juliet that he has heard the news and, like her, is desperate with worry. Juliet reveals to him that she is carrying a knife: if they can find no other way out of this dreadful marriage, she vows, she will take her own life without hesitation.

Racking his brains, the Friar hastily devises a plan. It is a rash and dangerous course of action, he warns Juliet, but, if successful, will both prevent her marriage to Paris and enable her to be with Romeo once more. Juliet demands to hear the plan; if it gives her the opportunity to be with her rightful husband, no danger will be too great.

> "... the speed of the plot carries everything along at such a pace that we feel the momentum cannot be checked; at this pace the smallest accident is fatal."
>
> M. C. Bradbrook, *Shakespeare and Elizabethan Poetry*, 1951

Searching hurriedly through his collection of potions and remedies, the Friar produces a little bottle. He instructs her to drink its contents tomorrow night, on the eve of her wedding. The effect, he warns, will be sudden and dramatic:

Friar Laurence . . . presently through all thy veins shall run
A cold and drowsy humour,[1] for no pulse
Shall keep his native[2] progress, but surcease:
No warmth, no breath shall testify thou livest,
The roses in thy lips and cheeks shall fade
To wanny[3] ashes, thy eyes' windows fall
Like death when he shuts up the day of life.

[1] *fluid*
[2] *natural, habitual*
[3] *pale*

It is in this death-like state that Juliet will be found on the morning of her wedding. She will then be carried away, in her finest clothes, as is the local tradition, and laid, uncovered, in the Capulets' burial-vault.

In the meantime, explains the Friar, he will send an urgent message to Romeo, instructing him to return to Verona at night and meet him by the tomb. The two of them will enter the vault and sit with Juliet as the effect of the potion wears off. Juliet will suffer no distress, feeling only as if she has woken from a pleasant sleep. When she is fully recovered, she and

Romeo can escape, under cover of darkness, and make their way together to Mantua.

Juliet agrees to the plan at once. She gratefully takes the phial containing the sleeping-potion, and leaves for home in good cheer. The Friar immediately sets about preparing a message for Romeo.

> ". . . the artifices of the play's style and structure create a condition of containment from which its energies break out with double force. Energies that explode on the slightest provocation into horse-play, sword-play, wordplay, love-play. . . . Behind all these energies, of course, releasing but at the same time shaping them, stands the energy of Shakespeare's own imagination, in sheer exuberance of creation melting down old forms to make them new."
>
> Maynard Mack, *Everybody's Shakespeare*, 1993

Urgent preparations begin

IV, ii

Lord Capulet is busy making arrangements for the forthcoming wedding. His resolution to hold a small, quiet ceremony has been forgotten: complaining that things will not be ready in time, he is hastily issuing invitations, and urgently trying to find enough cooks for the wedding-feast, now less than forty-eight hours away.

Juliet, returned from her visit to Friar Laurence, now enters. Her cheerful appearance, so different from her earlier wretchedness, attracts attention at once, and her words carry an even greater surprise:

Nurse	See where she comes from shrift with merry look.
Lord Capulet	How now, my headstrong: where have you been gadding?
Juliet	Where I have learnt me to repent the sin Of disobedient opposition To you and your behests . . . Henceforward I am ever rul'd by you.

As Juliet kneels in front of him, Capulet is overcome with delight. In a moment of impetuous excitement, he declares that the wedding will take place even sooner than planned:

Lord Capulet	Send for the County, go tell him of this. I'll have this knot knit up tomorrow morning.

Juliet mentions quickly that she met Paris at the Friar's cell earlier in the day; concerned that the Count may have found her behaviour less than friendly, she explains that her affection for him had to be tempered with modesty and restraint. Capulet approves thoroughly of Juliet's conduct, and is full of praise for the Friar, who has had such a benign influence on his daughter.

Juliet leaves, asking the Nurse to come and help her select her clothes for tomorrow's occasion. Her mother, unaware of the change of plan, is alarmed at the prospect of coping with so many guests at such short notice; it is already getting late. Capulet assures her that he will stay up all night to ensure that the preparations are complete:

Lord Capulet	We'll to church tomorrow.
Lady Capulet	We shall be short in our provision, 'Tis now near night.
Lord Capulet	Tush, I will stir about, And all things shall be well, I warrant thee, wife. Go thou to Juliet, help to deck up[1] her. I'll not to bed tonight . . .

> [1] *dress, adorn*

Capulet calls out for a servant to take the news to the Count, but there is no response. Realising that every single one is busy organising the festivities, he sets out himself, full of energy and exuberance:

Lord Capulet	Well, I will walk myself To County Paris, to prepare up him Against[1] tomorrow. My heart is wondrous light Since this same wayward girl is so reclaim'd.

> [1] *in anticipation of*

Juliet gathers her courage

IV, iii

It is late at night. Juliet, who has been trying on wedding-clothes with the Nurse's help, has made her choice. She asks the Nurse to leave: she has many prayers to say, she explains, and wishes to be alone until morning. Her mother comes to her room, anxious to help, but Juliet assures her that she is ready for the wedding, and asks to be left on her own.

As her mother leaves the room, Juliet experiences a sudden wave of panic, and she is on the verge of crying out for help. She quickly steadies herself:

Juliet   Farewell. God knows when we shall meet again.
I have a faint cold fear thrills through my veins
That almost freezes up the heat of life.
I'll call them back again to comfort me.
- Nurse! - What should she do here?
My dismal scene I needs must act alone.

Juliet picks up the phial and prepares to drink the Friar's potion. Doubts start flooding into her mind at once: perhaps it will have no effect, and she will have to go through with this hateful second marriage? She tucks a knife into her wedding-dress, determined to use it if the potion does not work.

Her imagination continues to race frantically, and a succession of horrifying thoughts runs through her mind: perhaps the potion is in fact a deadly poison, and the Friar is trying to cover up the fact that he has secretly married her to Romeo? Or perhaps she will awake in the stifling darkness of the vault before Romeo and the Friar arrive, and die of suffocation, or go mad with fear, surrounded by the bones of her ancestors and the rotting corpse of her cousin? Perhaps the vault is haunted?

The spirit of the dead Tybalt appears in her mind's eye, in

pursuit of his killer. She calls on him to leave her loved one in peace, and, with Romeo's name on her lips, drinks the potion. She collapses at once, unconscious, onto the bed.

"The sweetest and bitterest love and hatred, festive rejoicings and dark forebodings, tender embraces and sepulchral horrors . . . are all brought close to each other in this play; and yet these contrasts are so blended into a unity of impression, that the echo which the whole leaves in the mind resembles a single but endless sigh."

August Wilhelm von Schlegel, *Criticisms on Shakespeare's Tragedies*, 1811

A sleepless night

IV, iv

It is three in the morning, but the Capulet household is still a hive of activity. Preparations for the wedding-party, now only hours away, are in full swing.

In the kitchens they are busy roasting meat and baking cakes, and Lord Capulet is hovering around excitedly, giving instructions and hurrying everyone along. He rejects the Nurse's suggestion that he should go to bed. He has stayed awake all night many times in the past, he claims, and his wife teases him about the amorous prowling of his youth:

Nurse	Go, you cot-quean,[1] go,
	Get you to bed. Faith, you'll be sick tomorrow
	For this night's watching.[2]
Lord Capulet	No, not a whit. What, I have watch'd ere now
	All night for lesser cause, and ne'er been sick.
Lady Capulet	Ay, you have been a mouse-hunt[3] in your time;
	But I will watch you from such watching now.

[1] *man who interferes in domestic matters*
[2] *staying awake*
[3] *you have spent nights roving around looking for women*

Music is heard in the distance. Capulet realises that Paris is on his way, with a group of musicians to help the festivities along. He sends the Nurse off to wake Juliet and help her prepare for the ceremony.

Grief is visited upon the Capulets

IV, v

The Nurse enters Juliet's bedroom and calls out affectionately to the still figure on the bed. The girl needs all the sleep she can get before her wedding-night, reflects the Nurse, promptly asking for her lewdness to be forgiven:

Nurse   You take your pennyworths[1] now.
Sleep for a week; for the next night, I warrant,
The County Paris hath set up his rest[2]
That you shall rest but little! God forgive me!
Marry and amen. How sound is she asleep!

> [1] *whatever little amounts you can get*
> [2] *is banking on the fact*

Approaching Juliet to rouse her, the Nurse is surprised to see that, even though asleep, she is already dressed for the wedding. She comes closer, and is horror-stricken at the sight of Juliet's ashen face and motionless body. Her screams attract the attention of Lady Capulet, who rushes in and desperately begs the girl to wake up.

Lord Capulet now enters, unaware of the furore, calling for Juliet to hurry out and meet her bridegroom. His animated excitement vanishes as he surveys his daughter's pale, inert form:

Lord Capulet   She's cold,
Her blood is settled and her joints are stiff.
Life and these lips have long been separated.
Death lies on her like an untimely frost
Upon the sweetest flower of all the field.

As Capulet stands in silent anguish, and the women wail in misery, Count Paris arrives, bright and eager. Friar Laurence is with him, and the musicians follow, playing a cheerful, rousing chorus. The music comes to a halt as the visitors gather, grief-stricken, around Juliet's lifeless body.

Lord Capulet, his wife, Count Paris and the Nurse are all devastated, uncomprehending and angry at this sudden, inexplicable death. Their cries of mourning grow louder and more indignant until Friar Laurence, secretly aware that Juliet is drugged and not dead, interrupts. Juliet is in heaven, he tells them, and although it is natural for them to grieve they must behave with restraint and humility. As Capulet prepares sadly for the funeral rites, the Friar hints that there is a lesson to be learnt from this death:

Lord Capulet All things that we ordained festival
Turn from their office to black funeral:
Our instruments to melancholy bells,
Our wedding cheer to a sad burial feast;
Our solemn[1] hymns to sullen dirges change,
Our bridal flowers serve for a buried corse,[2]
And all things change them to the contrary.

Friar Laurence   . . . Every one prepare
To follow this fair corse unto her grave.
The heavens do lour upon you for some ill;[3]
Move them no more by crossing their high will.

[1] *celebratory*
[2] *corpse*
[3] *frown upon you for some sin you have committed*

Taking the flowers and the rosemary prepared for the wedding and casting them over Juliet's body, they carry her, in sorrowful procession, to the family's burial-vault.

News of Juliet reaches Mantua

V, i

Romeo has arrived in Mantua, his place of exile. He is hoping for news from Friar Laurence soon: eventually, perhaps, he may be able to return to Verona and his beloved Juliet. Although his situation is troublesome, he is in good spirits, heartened by a strange, potent dream of Juliet:

Romeo   I dreamt my lady came and found me dead . . .
And breath'd such life with kisses in my lips
That I reviv'd and was an emperor.

As Romeo reflects on the power of his love to bring him joy even in Juliet's absence, his manservant Balthasar rushes in. He has just travelled from Verona at breakneck speed. Romeo is pleased to see him: perhaps he has been sent by Friar Laurence to tell him of promising developments. He asks eagerly for word of Juliet and of his family.

Balthasar's news comes as a bolt from the blue. He has witnessed a tragic scene in the churchyard:

Balthasar   Her body sleeps in Capel's monument,
And her immortal part with angels lives.
I saw her laid low in her kindred's vault . . .

> *"To love extremely procureth either death or danger . . . From love, they lose themselves, their wits, and make shipwrack of their fortunes altogether . . . If this passion continue, it makes the blood hot, thick, and black; and if the inflammation get into the brain, with continual meditation and waking, it so dries it up, that madness follows, or else they make away themselves . . .*
>
> Robert Burton, *Anatomy of Melancholy*, 1621

For Romeo, there can only be one explanation for this final catastrophe. Fate itself is against his union with Juliet, and will do anything to keep them apart. He cries out defiantly against the stars: he will be with his wife even in death, he vows.

Balthasar is disturbed by the sudden frenzy that seems to have come over his master, and implores him to remain calm. Ignoring his pleas, Romeo orders him off to find some swift horses. His only remaining ambition is to be with Juliet as soon as possible, and to die by her side. He intends to ride back to Verona tonight, under cover of darkness, and make his way to her burial-place.

Casting about in his mind for a way to end his life, he suddenly remembers an apothecary's shop that earlier caught his attention. The owner was clearly impoverished and wretched, and in his shop was a sad, sparse display of remedies, perfumes and curios:

Romeo   Meagre were his looks,
          Sharp misery had worn him to the bones,
          And in his needy shop a tortoise hung,
          An alligator stuff'd, and other skins
          Of ill-shap'd fishes; and about his shelves
          A beggarly account[1] of empty boxes,
          Green earthen pots, bladders, and musty seeds,
          Remnants of packthread,[2] and old cakes of
               roses[3]
          Were thinly scatter'd to make up a show.

[1] *pathetic number*
[2] *string used for tying bundles*
[3] *pressed rose-petals*

From amongst his drugs and potions, Romeo is sure that the apothecary can supply him with what he needs. He finds himself outside the shop: discovering that it is closed, he bangs on the locked door, and calls out impatiently until the apothecary, startled by the commotion, appears.

Romeo, wasting no time on explanations or excuses, makes a blunt demand: he wants some effective, deadly poison, enough to guarantee the immediate death of anyone who takes it. In return, he offers the apothecary a small fortune in gold, more than enough to relieve the man's poverty for the rest of his life.

The apothecary tells Romeo that he does indeed possess such a poison, but its sale is strictly forbidden in Mantua, on pain of death. Romeo brushes aside the man's objections:

Romeo   Famine is in thy cheeks,
                    Need and oppression starveth in thy eyes,
                    Contempt and beggary hangs upon thy back.
                    The world is not thy friend, nor the world's
                        law;
                    The world affords no law to make thee rich;
                    Then be not poor, but break it, and take this.[1]

Apothecary   My poverty, but not my will consents.

Romeo   I pay thy poverty and not thy will.

      [1] *break the law, and take my gold*

The apothecary hands Romeo the poison, assuring him that it will bring about the instant death of anyone who drinks it. In return, Romeo gives him the promised gold, which he now regards as useless and pernicious:

Romeo   There is thy gold - worse poison to men's souls,
                    Doing more murder in this loathsome world
                    Than these poor compounds that thou mayst
                        not sell.

Romeo leaves with his poison, ready to set off for Verona and Juliet's tomb.

The Friar's plan miscarries

V, ii

A visitor arrives at Friar Laurence's cell. It is Friar John, who had been entrusted by Friar Laurence with the delivery of his letter to Romeo.

The letter told Romeo of the plan for Juliet to take the sleeping-potion, explaining that she would be laid, apparently dead, in the Capulets' burial-vault. It also instructed Romeo to return to Verona at night and meet Friar Laurence at the vault, where they would watch over Juliet as she recovered from the potion, and from where Romeo would take her secretly back to Mantua.

". . . a populous city, confined by the protection of its own walls, breeds a stifling atmosphere with its own kinds of fearful menace. Elizabethan Londoners needed no reminder that the infectious heat of summer can have fatal consequences in cities, and indeed there would be for an Elizabethan audience a cruelly familiar plausibility, as well as an apt symbolic significance, in the outbreak of plague which prevents Friar John from getting through to Romeo with the fateful message."

Brian Gibbons, Introduction to the Arden edition of *Romeo and Juliet*, 1980

Outbreaks of bubonic plague were a regular occurrence in England, and particularly in London, in Shakespeare's time.

When there was a severe epidemic - with more than thirty deaths a week - the theatres were closed down by the authorities, who believed, probably correctly, that large public assemblies helped to spread the infection. Unfortunately for

Friar John brings disturbing news. Before setting out from Verona, he had stopped to call on a fellow-friar who was to accompany him - as required by the Franciscan order - on his journey. His companion was visiting the sick, and Friar John joined him at a sufferer's house. The two of them were about to leave for Mantua when misfortune struck:

the acting companies, the disease tended to be at its most virulent during the summer, when the theatres - which had no lighting or heating - did most of their business.

In 1592, a particularly serious and prolonged epidemic of the plague resulted in the closure of the London theatres for two years. The acting companies were thrown into turmoil; many were disbanded, while some unsuccessful attempts were made to tour the provinces. During this time, Shakespeare seems to have turned to poetry, with works such as *Venus and Adonis* and a number of Sonnets. In 1594, with the worst of the outbreak over, the acting companies regrouped, and Shakespeare joined the newly-formed Chamberlain's Men, with whom he was to stay for the rest of his career. One of the first successes of this new company, helping to establish it as the foremost acting troupe in England, was Shakespeare's early masterpiece, *Romeo and Juliet.*

Friar John   . . . the searchers[1] of the town,
                    Suspecting that we both were in a house
                    Where the infectious pestilence[2] did reign,
                    Seal'd up the doors and would not let us forth,
                    So that my speed to Mantua there was stay'd.[3]

> [1] *officials authorised to discover cases of plague, and*
>   *prevent the spread of the disease*
> [2] *plague*
> [3] *my progress to Mantua was prevented*

Friar John was not even allowed to pass his letter out of the sealed house: he has only just been released himself, and the letter to Romeo remains undelivered.

Friar Laurence, alarmed, orders his fellow-friar to find him an iron crowbar at once. He must make his way to the Capulets' tomb; Juliet will be waking from her deep slumber soon, and without Friar Laurence's message Romeo will not be there as planned to comfort her.

Paris's mourning is disturbed

V, iii

Late at night, two visitors arrive at the silent churchyard where Juliet's body has been laid to rest. The two men making their way through the graves in the darkness are Count Paris and his page.

Paris has come to lay flowers and sprinkle perfumed water at the tomb of his adored Juliet, snatched away from him only hours before their wedding. Wishing to be alone as he carries out his funeral rites, he instructs his page to wait behind and listen intently, and tells him to whistle if he hears footsteps anywhere in the churchyard. He then approaches the Capulets' burial-vault and speaks to his beloved, promising that he will be present every night to honour her memory:

Paris   Sweet flower, with flowers thy bridal bed I
            strew.
         O woe, thy canopy[1] is dust and stones
         Which with sweet water nightly I will dew,
         Or wanting that, with tears distill'd by moans.
         The obsequies[2] that I for thee will keep
         Nightly shall be to strew thy grave and weep.

[1]   awning, covering suspended over the bridal bed
[2]   funeral observances

Hearing a whistle from his page, Paris retreats into the darkness, perplexed and angry at this intrusion. The newcomer is Romeo, rushing impetuously towards the tomb by torchlight, followed by his servant Balthasar.

Romeo grabs hold of the tools that Balthasar has been carrying, and hands him a letter, telling him to deliver it to his father in the morning. He then tells Balthasar that he is about to enter the tomb for a glimpse of Juliet. He issues a stern warning: whatever Balthasar may see or hear, he must stay away. In his present ruthless mood, Romeo will slaughter him without hesitation if he allows his curiosity to get the better of him and approaches the tomb. Balthasar agrees to leave him undisturbed, and Romeo bids him farewell, rewarding him with gold.

Taking hold of the burning torch, Romeo approaches the door of the burial-vault. Balthasar, in the meantime, hides nearby: despite his promise, he is loath to leave his master in his present state. Romeo attacks the door of the tomb with a crowbar and pickaxe, and manages to wrench it open.

As Romeo is about to enter the burial-chamber itself, Paris, horrified at this desecration of Juliet's grave, leaps out of the darkness and confronts him. He recognises the young Montague, knowing him to be Tybalt's killer, banished on pain of death for his crime. Paris fears that he has returned to carry his hostility for the Capulets to even more barbarous depths:

Paris   This is that banish'd haughty Montague
That murder'd my love's cousin - with which grief
It is supposed the fair creature died -
And here is come to do some villainous shame
To the dead bodies . . .
Can vengeance be pursu'd further than death?
Condemned villain, I do apprehend[1] thee.
Obey, and go with me, for thou must die.

    [1] *arrest*

Consumed by his determination to be with Juliet, Romeo takes no interest in the intruder's identity. Unmoved by his threat, he tells him to leave at once. He is resolved on his course of action: if the stranger interferes, he warns, he is likely to provoke Romeo to a murderous fury.

> *"Romeo and Paris seek manhood through love rather than fighting, but are finally impelled by the feud to fight each other."*
>
> Coppélia Kahn, *Coming of Age in Verona*, 1977

Romeo descends into the grave

Paris stands his ground, and repeats that he intends to arrest Romeo for his unlawful return to Verona. Romeo responds immediately and savagely, attacking the stranger in a sudden rage. Paris's page, witnessing the violent encounter, races off to find the night watchmen.

The struggle between the two men is quickly over; and Romeo's opponent, with his dying breath, asks to be laid in the tomb next to Juliet. Romeo, his fit of fury disappearing as suddenly as it came, now gazes calmly at the face of his victim. Realising who it is, he feels a pang of sympathy, half-remembering something that Balthasar had told him as they were riding hastily back to Verona:

Romeo   Let me peruse this face.
       Mercutio's kinsman, noble County Paris!
       What said my man, when my betossed[1] soul
       Did not attend him, as we rode? I think
       He told me Paris should have married Juliet.
       Said he not so? Or did I dream it so?
                 . . . O, give me thy hand,
       One writ with me in sour misfortune's book.
       I'll bury thee in a triumphant grave.

     [1]   *agitated, turbulent*

Romeo enters the mouth of the tomb, dragging Paris's corpse with him and laying it in the vault. He now approaches Juliet's body. She is in her bridal clothes, and Romeo marvels at her radiance:

Romeo   O my love, my wife,
Death that hath suck'd the honey of thy breath
Hath had no power yet upon thy beauty.
Thou art not conquer'd. Beauty's ensign[1] yet
Is crimson in thy lips and in thy cheeks,
And Death's pale flag is not advanced there.

[1] *flag, banner*

Looking around him, Romeo sees the bloody corpse of Tybalt lying nearby. He asks his forgiveness, and promises that atonement for his untimely death is at hand. He turns again, finally, to Juliet. The time has come to join her in death:

Romeo   O here
Will I set up my everlasting rest[1]
And shake the yoke of inauspicious stars
From this world-wearied flesh. Eyes, look your
        last.
Arms, take your last embrace! And lips, O you
The doors of breath, seal with a righteous kiss
A dateless bargain[2] to engrossing[3] Death.

[1] *make my permanent home*
[2] *an everlasting contract*
[3] *devouring, all-consuming; monopolising*

Romeo takes out the phial of poison obtained from the apothecary in Mantua. As he drinks, he calls on the poison to guide him successfully to destruction, and gives his beloved a last tender kiss:

Romeo   Come, bitter conduct,[1] come unsavoury guide,
Thou desperate pilot, now at once run[2] on
The dashing rocks thy seasick weary bark.[3]
Here's to my love! [*He drinks.*] O true apothecary,
Thy drugs are quick. Thus with a kiss I die.

[1] *escort*
[2] *crash, wreck*
[3] *ship, Romeo's body*

As Romeo collapses, dying, there is another visitor to the churchyard. Friar Laurence has come to rescue Juliet. Carrying a lantern, and weighed down with tools for opening the vault, he hurries towards the Capulets' tomb, stumbling over graves in his haste.

Juliet stays with Romeo

The Friar comes across Romeo's manservant Balthasar, who has been lying low in the darkness. Surprised to see a torch burning in one of the vaults nearby, the Friar asks Balthasar whether it is in the Capulets' tomb. The man confirms that it is; moreover, his master Romeo has entered the vault.

Friar Laurence, shocked to hear that Romeo is present, and fearful that some dreadful misfortune has come about, asks the man to come with him and investigate. Balthasar refuses adamantly; Romeo has threatened him with death if he comes near. Apprehensive, Friar Laurence approaches the Capulets' tomb on his own.

> *"The Friar, coming to this death-scene, comes a moment too late. Juliet wakes from her trance a moment too late. Theirs are the only delays in this drama of fever . . ."*
>
> John Masefield, *William Shakespeare*, 1911

To the Friar's horror, he finds that his fears are more than justified. The door of the vault has been wrenched off: there are two swords nearby, and blood is spattered around the mouth of the tomb. Looking inside the vault, the Friar is confronted by the harrowing sight of the corpses of Romeo and Paris lying near Juliet, the one pale, the other gashed and bloody.

As Friar Laurence looks on, Juliet stirs: the effect of the potion is wearing off and, as the Friar had predicted, she awakens refreshed and alert, as if from a sound sleep. Realising that she is in the burial-vault, as planned, Juliet is calm and unafraid, unaware as yet of the bodies nearby. Seeing the Friar at the entrance, she asks at once for word of Romeo.

The Friar hastily breaks the dreadful news. As a last resort, he implores her to come to a place of shelter and secrecy, away from these appalling events and their aftermath. There is no time to lose:

Friar Laurence   Lady, come from that nest
Of death, contagion, and unnatural sleep.
A greater power than we can contradict
Hath thwarted our intents. Come, come away.
Thy husband in thy bosom there lies dead,
And Paris too. Come, I'll dispose of thee
Among a sisterhood of holy nuns.
Stay not to question, for the Watch[1] is coming.

---

[1] *night watchmen, officers of the law*

Juliet refuses to join the Friar as he hurries off into the night. She resolves to die, here and now, next to Romeo. She notices the phial of poison, but discovers that it is empty. As she kisses her husband she realises that he has only just died:

Juliet   Drunk all, and left no friendly drop
                 To help me after?[1] I will kiss thy lips.
                 Haply[2] some poison yet doth hang on them
                 To make me die with a restorative.[3]
                 Thy lips are warm!

[1] *to follow you*
[2] *perhaps*
[3] *reviving kiss*

"Romeo and Juliet *is a tragedy of first love. For these young lovers, in their abandon, the world does not exist. That is, perhaps, why they choose death so easily."*

Jan Kott, *Shakespeare Our Contemporary*, 1965

Some night watchmen, summoned by Paris's page, now arrive at the churchyard. Juliet, hearing them approach, acts quickly. She remembers the knife that she concealed in her wedding-dress, when she had feared that the Friar's potion might not have its desired effect. It was to be her last resort as a means of escaping an unwanted marriage; now that her true husband is dead, it must serve to unite the two of them in death:

Juliet   Yea, noise? Then I'll be brief. O happy[1] dagger.
                This[2] is thy sheath. There rust, and let me die.

[1] *opportune*
[2] *my body*

The truth is revealed

Paris's page leads one of the watchmen to the Capulets' vault,
in which the torch is still burning. The watchman is shocked
at the sight of the corpses: and he is mystified to discover that
Juliet, buried some time ago, has only been dead for a matter
of minutes, apparently from a stab wound.

The watchman orders some of his fellow-officers to search
the churchyard. Anyone they find is to be arrested and brought
forward for questioning. Some other officers are sent off to awaken
the families of the dead, and to summon the Prince to the scene
of the tragedy.

Balthasar is apprehended by the watchmen and brought to
the tomb. The Friar is soon arrested too, shaking and weeping.
Still carrying the spade and other tools with which he had in-
tended to free Juliet, he is regarded at once with suspicion.

Prince Escalus, with his guards and attendants, now comes
into the churchyard and approaches the tomb, demanding to
know why he has been summoned at such an early hour.

The Capulets are next to make their way through the darkness towards the light of the open vault. The sight of their
daughter, blood still flowing from her fatal stab wound, is almost too painful to bear. Capulet assumes that Romeo, lying
next to her, was her murderer:

Lord Capulet O heavens! O wife, look how our daughter
                     bleeds!
                  This dagger hath mista'en, for lo, his house[1]
                  Is empty on the back of Montague,
                  And it mis-sheathed in my daughter's bosom.
Lady Capulet O me! This sight of death is as a bell
                  That warns my old age to a sepulchre.[2]

    [1] *its rightful place*
    [2] *grave*

Lord Montague now arrives, already heavy with grief; his wife has died, only a few hours ago, heartbroken at Romeo's banishment from Verona. The sight of his son, lifeless and pale in the torchlit vault, leaves him utterly defeated.

The Prince, whose kinsman Paris is also lying dead in the vault, calls for restraint and patience: the first priority is to establish how these terrible deaths have come about. Friar Laurence steps forward, aware that he is under the heaviest suspicion. He promises to be brief; exhausted and dejected, he feels that his own death is close at hand.

The Friar first reveals, to everyone's astonishment, that Romeo and Juliet were man and wife, and that he himself officiated at their wedding. He recounts how Romeo's banishment, rather than Tybalt's death, had caused Juliet such distress, worsened by the prospect of marriage to Paris: to prevent her immediate suicide, he had proposed the plan of using the potion to feign her death. The message telling Romeo of the plan did not arrive, explains the Friar, and when he came to rescue Juliet from the burial-vault he found it open, with Paris and Romeo already dead. Juliet, refusing to escape with him, has evidently taken her own life.

Juliet's Nurse can confirm the fact of the secret marriage, says the Friar. He submits himself to the Prince for judgement, ready to face death:

Friar Laurence   . . . if aught in this
                        Miscarried by my fault, let my old life
                        Be sacrific'd some hour before his time
                        Unto the rigour of severest law.

Prince Escalus reassures Friar Laurence that he is confident of his integrity. He then turns to Balthasar, who describes Romeo's impetuous return to Verona on hearing of Juliet's death. Just before he entered the tomb, Romeo had given Balthasar a letter to be delivered to his father, Lord Montague: the Prince demands to see it.

Paris's page, who first called for the night watchmen, is now brought before the Prince. He describes Romeo's sudden intrusion as Paris was laying flowers by the tomb, and the ensuing struggle.

A time to mourn

The Prince reads Romeo's final letter to his father, which confirms everything that the Friar has said, and reveals Romeo's chosen means of dying. He calls Capulet and Montague before him:

Prince   ... here he writes that he did buy a poison
Of a poor pothecary, and therewithal
Came to this vault to die and lie with Juliet.
Where be these enemies? Capulet, Montague,
See what a scourge is laid upon your hate,
That heaven finds means to kill your joys[1] with
    love;
And I, for winking[2] at your discords too,
Have lost a brace[3] of kinsmen. All are punish'd.

[1]   *children*
[2]   *turning a blind eye, tolerating*
[3]   *pair*

There have been too many deaths; their feud has even turned love to death. Romeo and Juliet, Tybalt, and his own kinsmen Mercutio and Paris are all dead, and the older generation, racked with grief, is hastening towards an early grave.

Capulet offers Montague his hand: the only dowry that can be offered for the marriage of their two children is the handshake of friendship and reconciliation. Taking his hand, Montague proposes a rich and lasting memorial to Capulet's daughter, and Lord Capulet promises the same for Romeo:

Lord Montague   ... I will raise her statue in pure gold,
That[1] whiles Verona by that name is known,
There shall no figure at such rate[2] be set
As that of true and faithful Juliet.
Lord Capulet   As rich shall Romeo's by his lady lie,
Poor sacrifices of our enmity.

[1]   *so that*
[2]   *value, esteem*

> *". . . it is because there has been so much hate in Verona that love, a counterpoint, springs up; and is sacrificed; and brings peace to the city. And in four days."*
>
> Karolous Koun, director of *Romeo and Juliet* at the Royal Shakespeare Theatre, 1967

The Prince looks up at the heavens. Daybreak has come, but the skies are overcast: there is no sun this morning. The time for judgement will come in due course. For the present, the living must mourn the dead, and reflect on what has happened:

Prince   A glooming peace this morning with it brings:
The sun for sorrow will not show his head.
Go hence to have more talk of these sad things.
Some shall be pardon'd, and some punished,
For never was a story of more woe
Than this of Juliet and her Romeo.

In the grey light of dawn a sombre procession makes its way, slowly and silently, past the graves, through the desolate churchyard, back towards the city.

ACKNOWLEDGEMENTS

The following publications have proved invaluable as sources of factual information and critical insight:

Charles Boyce, *Shakespeare A to Z*, Roundtable Press, 1990

M. C. Bradbrook, *Shakespeare and Elizabethan Poetry*, Chatto & Windus, 1951

Brenda Bruce, *Playing the Nurse*, from *Players of Shakespeare*, edited by Philip Brockbank, Cambridge University Press, 1985

J. A. Bryant Jr, Introduction to the Signet Classic Shakespeare edition of *Romeo and Juliet*, New American Library, 1964

Northrop Frye, *On Shakespeare*, Yale University Press, 1986

Brian Gibbons, Introduction to the Arden Shakespeare edition of *Romeo and Juliet*, Methuen, 1980

Germaine Greer, *Shakespeare*, from the *Past Masters* series, edited by Keith Thomas, Oxford University Press, 1986

Coppélia Kahn, *Coming of Age in Verona*, Modern Language Studies, 1977

Jan Kott, *Shakespeare Our Contemporary*, Doubleday, 1965

Maynard Mack, *Everybody's Shakespeare*, Bison Books, 1993

John Masefield, *William Shakespeare*, Thornton Butterworth, 1911

Susan Snyder, *Romeo and Juliet: Comedy into Tragedy*, Essays in Criticism, 1970

T. J. B. Spencer, Introduction to the New Penguin Shakespeare edition of *Romeo and Juliet*, Penguin, 1967

Caroline Spurgeon, *Shakespeare's Imagery and What It Tells Us*, Cambridge University Press, 1935

John Wain, *The Living World of Shakespeare: A Playgoer's Guide*, Macmillan, 1964

Stanley Wells, *Shakespeare: A Dramatic Life*, Sinclair-Stevenson, 1994

All quotations from *Romeo and Juliet* are taken from the Arden Shakespeare.